The Violin, How it Works

The Violin, How it Works

A Practical Guide to Violin Ownership

Michael J. Pagliaro

Co-Published in Partnership with the
National Association for Music Education

ROWMAN & LITTLEFIELD
Lanham • Boulder • New York • London

Published by Rowman & Littlefield
An imprint of The Rowman & Littlefield Publishing Group, Inc.
4501 Forbes Boulevard, Suite 200, Lanham, Maryland 20706
www.rowman.com

86-90 Paul Street, London EC2A 4NE, United Kingdom

British Library Cataloguing in Publication Information Available

Library of Congress Cataloging-in-Publication Data

ISBN 9781475868128 (paper : alk. paper) | ISBN 9781475868135 (electronic)

∞™ The paper used in this publication meets the minimum requirements of American National Standard for Information Sciences—Permanence of Paper for Printed Library Materials, ANSI/NISO Z39.48-1992.

Table of Contents

Acknowledgments	vi
Introduction	vii
1. What Are the Parts of My Violin and How Do They Work?	1
2. How Do I Care for My Violin Outfit?	17
3. How Should I Plan My Practice Sessions?	29
4. What Items (Accessories) Will I Need to Help Me Play My Violin?	33
5. How Are Violins Made?	45
6. What Is the History of the Violin?	63
7. How Are Violin Bows Made?	75
8. What Is the History of Violin Bows?	83
9. A Dictionary for Violin Students	87
Index	95

Acknowledgments

The following extraordinarily gifted professionals in the field of musical instrument fabrication and distribution have generously granted permission to use information and artwork from their websites. Listed in alphabetical order they are:

Donna Altieri Bags, info@altieribags.com;
Dr. Robin Deverich, for allowing the use of
The Advanced Fingering Chart 1st - 7th Positions www.Violinonline.com;
Scott Hershey, master luthier at http://www.hersheyviolins.net;
Eitan Hoffer, archetier extraordinaire, specialist in the
fabrication of ancient bows at http://www.hoffer-bows.com;
Lars Kirmser, publisher and musical instrument specialist at
http://www.musictrader.com;
Jimmy Sang Wang, bow manufacturer at http://www.wangbow.com;
Otis A. Tomas, master luthier at www.otis@fiddletree.com;

Introduction

The method book you are already using was written to help you learn how to play the violin. That book contains information on how to hold your violin, make a sound, read music, how to play the different notes, and much more.

This companion book will teach you additional information about your instrument that will help you better understand how it works, how to work it, care for it, and how to be a more knowledgeable violinist.

The first section of this companion book is a review of information that might be on the first few pages of your method book. Even if you know that information, spend a few moments reading the section to see if you can find something you did not yet learn. From there on, you will be learning information about the violin that not too many students will ever know.

You do not have to read this book in the order in which the chapters appear. Start at any chapter that may interest you and then, as you progress, move around to the chapters that are related to your violin studies as you progress.

Note: The following is an explanation of a system used throughout all of music study called ***Scientific Pitch Notation***. This a valuable tool which can serve you throughout your music career.

Scientific Pitch Notation helps you to know exactly where a note is located on the staff without having to see the note in print. This system uses a combination of letters and numerals (alphanumeric) to tell you exactly where a note is in the entire range of notes. An example would be middle C whose alphanumeric name is C4. The C one octave below middle C is C3. The C an octave above middle C is C5. The notes going up between these Cs keep the C's numeral until the next C is reached. An example would be C4, D4, E4, F4, G4, A4, B4, C5, D5, etc. The figure below shows the alphanumeric symbol for all notes.

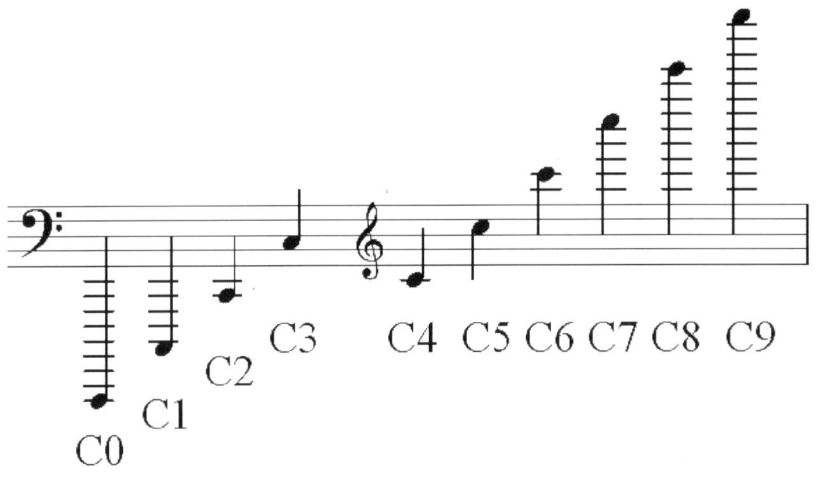

Chapter 1

What Are the Parts of My Violin and How Do They Work?

Lesson One

Violin Parts

Let's begin by learning the names of some of the parts of your violin. Using the picture below along with your own violin, locate the parts named:

1. strings
2. bridge
3. top
4. sound post (inside)
5. back

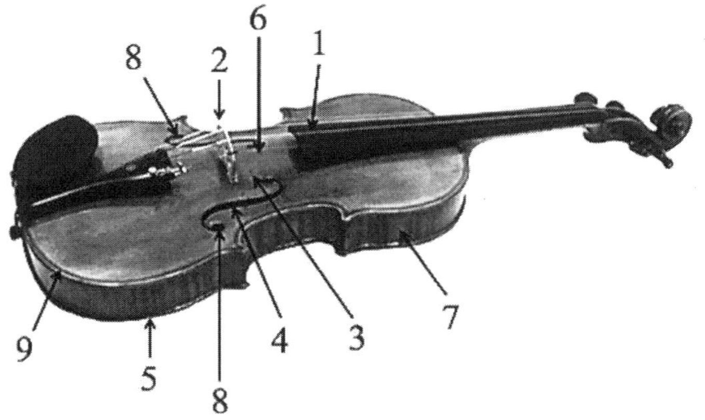

6. bass bar (inside top)
7. sides
8. "*f*" hole
9. purfling

Next are the names of the parts that support the strings. Some parts are repeated. Starting from the top of the instrument, you have the:

A. scroll
B. peg box
C. pegs
D. neck
E. fingerboard
F. bridge
G. chin rest

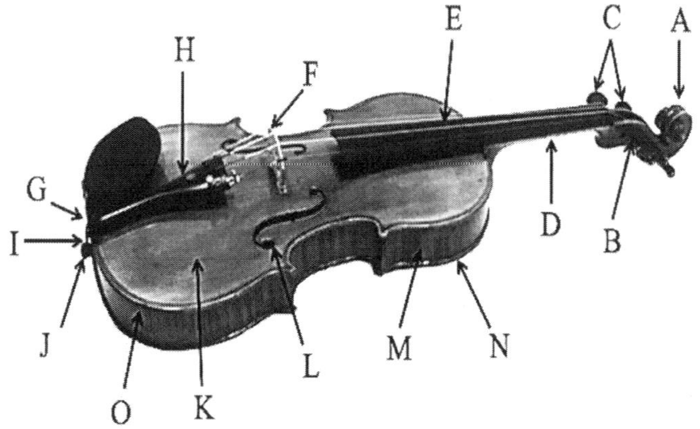

H. tail piece
I. tail gut
J. end button
K. top
L. "*f*" hole
M. side
N. back
O. purfling

Let's look inside your violin.

Supporting the top and back of your violin are the:

A. ribs and linings
B. top and bottom blocks
C. corner blocks
D. bass bar
E. sound post

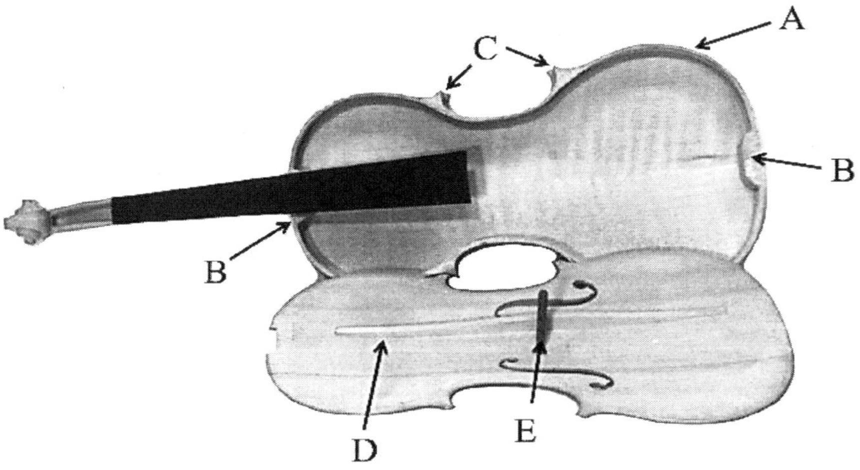

All the inside parts work together to strengthen the sound that you hear as you bow or pluck a string.

Lesson Two

How Do the Parts Work?

The Bridge — The sound you produce when you pluck or bow a string travels to the feet of the bridge, and then through to the top of your violin.

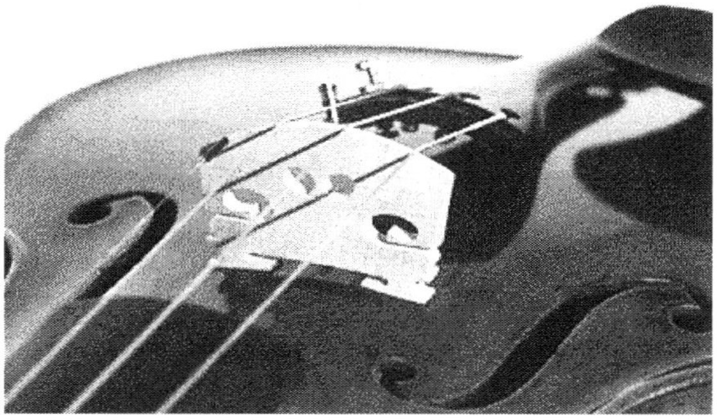

"f"* Holes** — "*f*" holes are the f-shaped holes that are cut into the top of your violin. There is one ***"f" hole on either side of the bridge.

These ***"f"*** shaped openings let out the sound that is vibrating inside the body of your violin.

The Sound Post— The sound post is inside the body of your violin. Look inside through the "*f*" hole on the E string side.

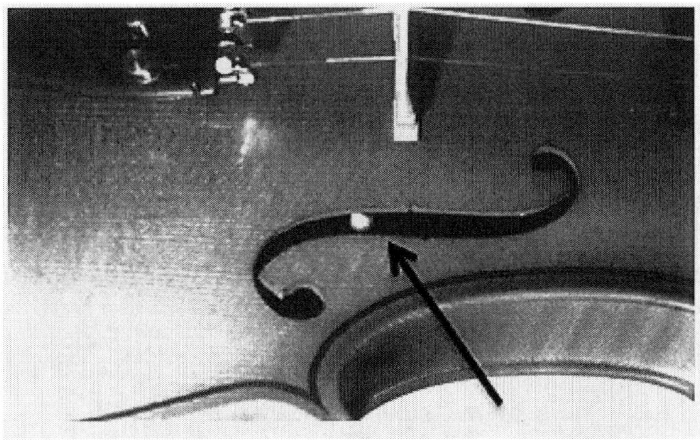

The sound post is made of soft wood. It supports the top of your violin and sends the sound of the high notes from the top of the instrument to its back.

The Bass Bar —The bass bar is on the underside of the top of your violin beneath the bridge foot on the G string side. The bass bar strengthens your violin's top while carrying the lower notes throughout the top of the instrument. You can see a bass bar by placing a dental mirror in the ***"f"*** hole on the G string side of your instrument.

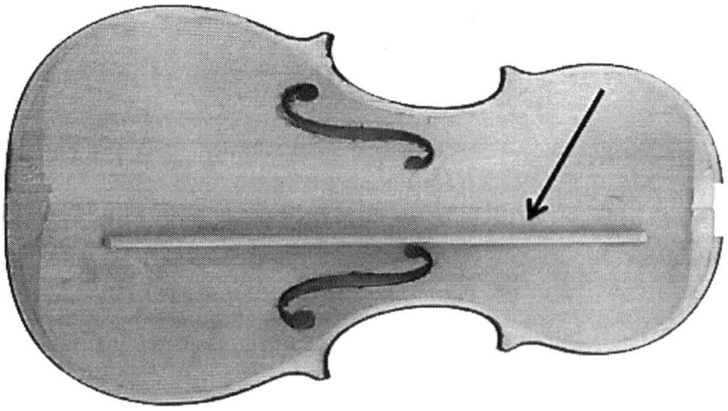

The combination of the bridge, sound post, and bass bar with the top and back of your violin produce the sound that you hear when you bow or pluck a string.

The Sides and Back — The sides and back of your violin hold the instrument together.

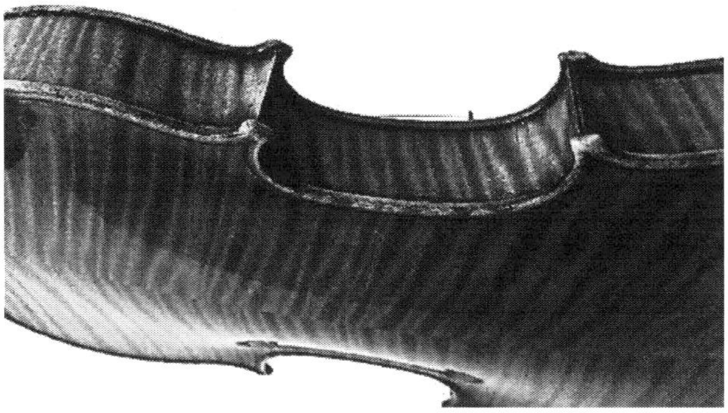

These parts are made of maple wood which is very strong. The strength is needed to support the pressure that the tightened strings put on the top of your violin. When all four strings are tuned, the pressure they put on the instrument is equal to about 68 pounds, the weight of a pile of almost 45 iPads.

Purfling — Two parallel strips of ebony, a dark hard wood, are inserted into the surface around the edge of the top and back of your violin.

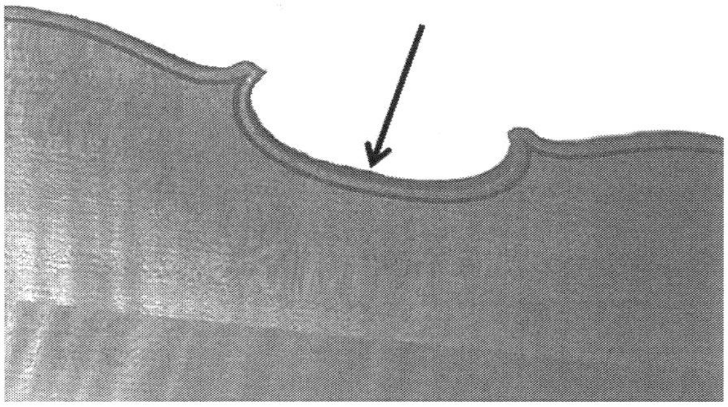

These two strips of wood are called purfling. They outline the area that will vibrate on the top and back of your violin. They also add strength to the edges of the instrument's body.

Lesson Three

The Sound Voyage

Using the same picture where you learned the names of your violin's parts, let's follow the trip sound makes throughout your violin as you play.

When you bow or pluck a string (1)

its motion (vibration) is picked up by the bridge (2)

and sent to the top of the violin (3).

That vibration travels to the sound post (4)

which then carries the vibration to the violin's back (5)

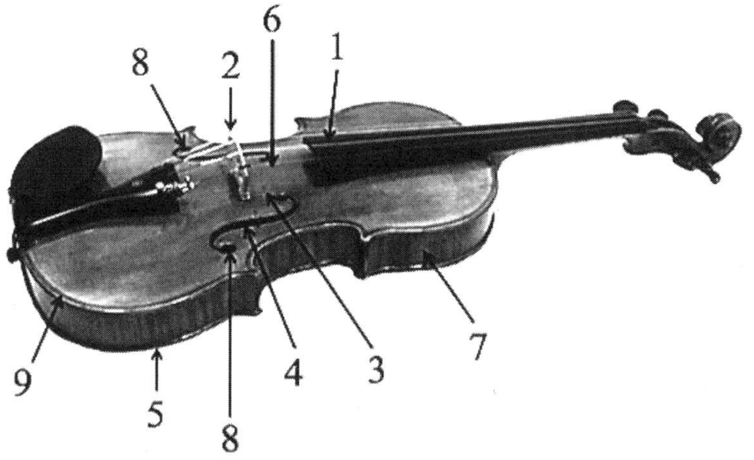

and is spread throughout the top of the violin by the bass bar (6).

The top and back of the violin are supported by its sides (7).

The motion of all these parts sets the air inside the violin's body into a pumping action that forces the sound out through the ***"f"*** holes (8).

The small wooden strips called purfling (9) around the edge of the violin control the vibration of sound throughout the top and back and give strength to their edges.

Lesson Four

Tuning Your Violin

Tuning your violin will be easy if you understand how the pegs and fine tuners work.

The violin has wedge-shaped (narrower at one end than the other) wooden pegs which are forced into holes in the peg box.

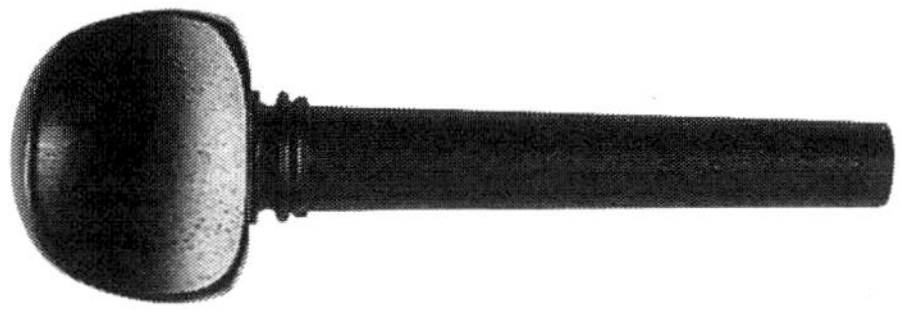

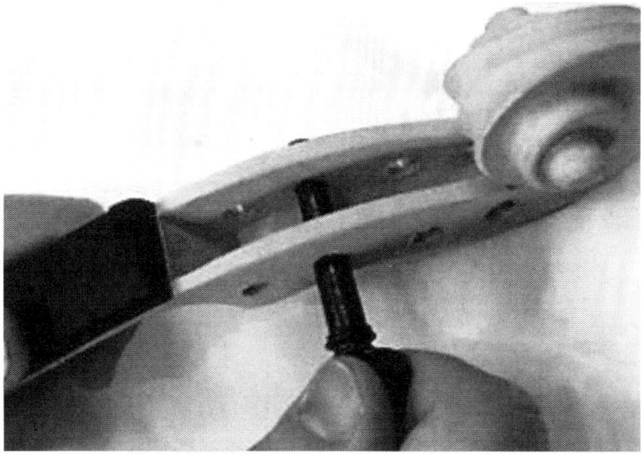

The term pitch refers to how high or low a note is. To tune your violin, you will need to hear the correct pitch for each string. The open strings on a violin are pictured below.

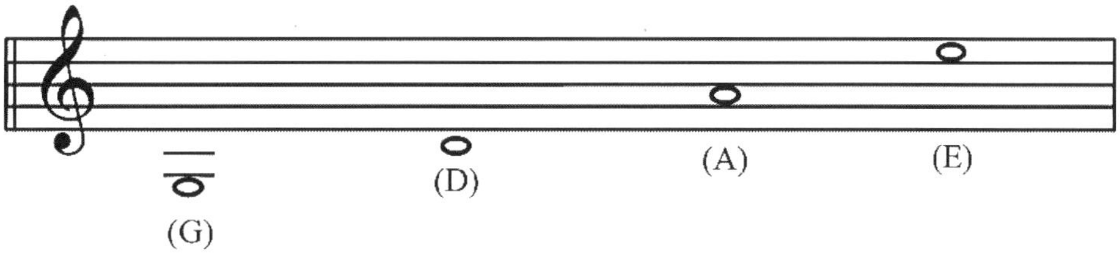

You can get the correct sounds for the G, D, A, and E from a piano, a pitch pipe or electronic tuner (pictured below). These are just some of the many different kinds of tuning aids you can use. (See chapter 4 on violin accessories for more information on these devices.)

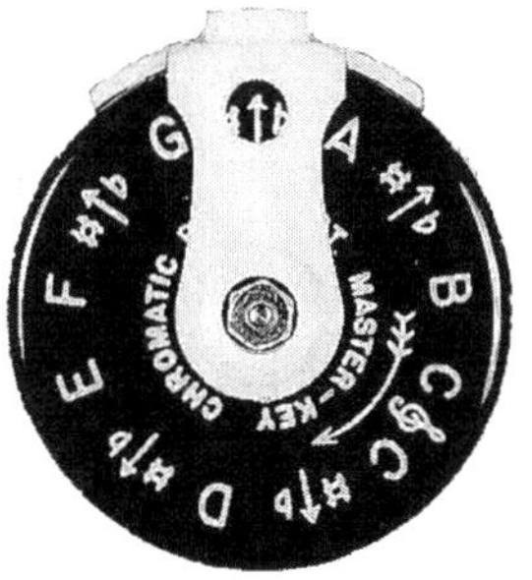

You can also Google <u>*YouTube tuning a violin*</u> where you will find several videos that will help you do a perfect job of tuning your violin.

To tune your violin successfully:

1. Hold the instrument on your lap with the scroll up and the strings facing you.

2. Select the pitch you need (G, D, A, or E) for the string you are tuning.

3. Sound the pitch on the tuning device and try to fix that sound in your mind. Singing the pitch with the tuner will help.

4. When you have the pitch firmly fixed in your mind, pluck the string to be tuned.

5. While the string is sounding the note you have just plucked, *slowly* tighten the string by turning the peg toward the top of the scroll, and, as you turn the peg, *push it in* so that it is forced into the holes of the peg box.

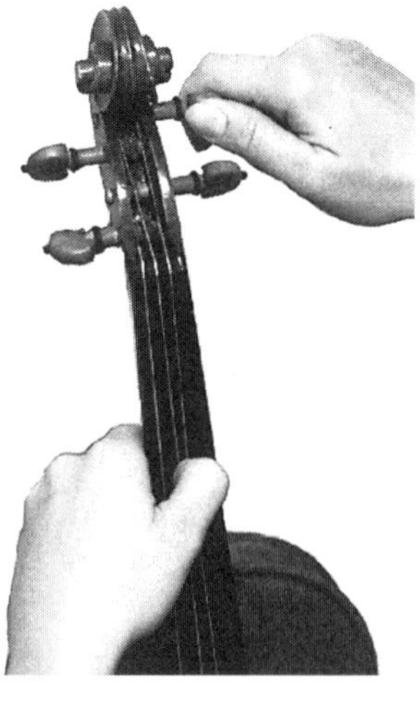

6. This picture shows how to turn and push in the peg as you tune. *It is very important that you force the peg into the peg holes.* If you just turn the peg, it will not hold the string in tune.

7. While you are slowly turning and pushing the peg in, continue to pluck the string, listening to the sound getting higher. When it reaches the pitch you have in mind, stop. The string will be tuned.

8. If you need to adjust the pitch just a tiny bit more, you can do so using small screws on the fine tuner on the tailpiece. These will raise or lower the pitch in small amounts.

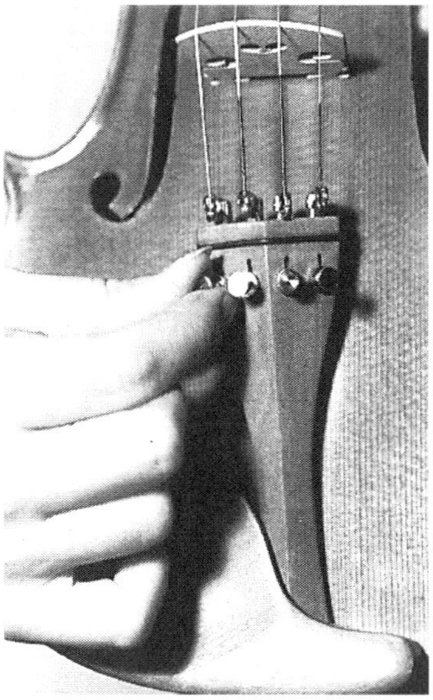

9. With the instrument facing you, pluck the string again while you turn the fine tuner to the right to raise the pitch or to the left to lower the pitch.

Lesson Five

Your Bow

The Bow — The violin bow is easily identified by the square back of the frog (arrow).

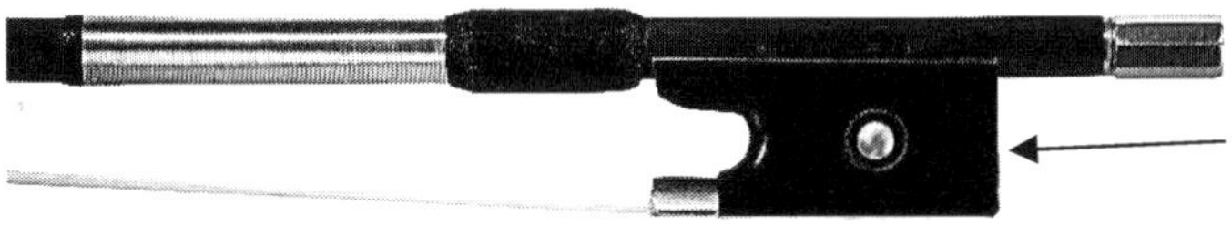

Using your method book with your teacher's help, you have learned how to hold and use a bow. Now let's learn about the parts of a bow and how it makes the sounds you are playing. Begin by learning the parts of the bow so that you can better care for and use it.

A bow is made up of about 175 hairs connected to a stick.

Bow Hair — The hair used on violin bows can be taken from the tail of a horse or can be manmade. Horse hair is the better choice but there is also some very good manmade (synthetic) bow hair in use.

If you take a close look at bow hair, you will think that it is smooth. But if you look at bow hair under a microscope, you will be surprised to see that the surface is actually rough. The picture below shows a magnified horse hair.

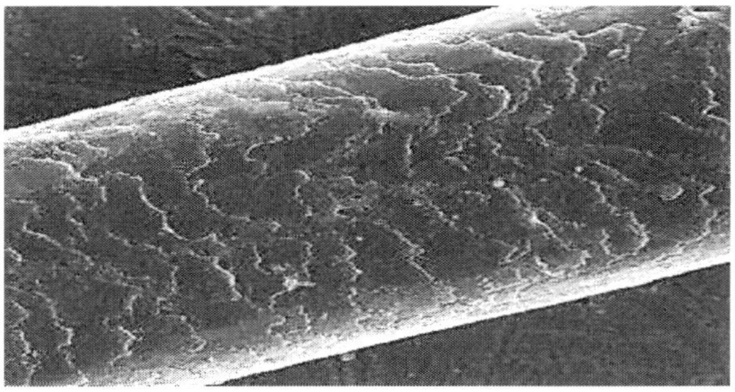

Bow Hair under a Microscope

This rough surface along with violin rosin that you apply to the hair catches on to a string causing it to vibrate and make sound.

Bow Parts — The diagram below shows how the hair is connected to the bow stick.

The end of the bow hair (A) is wedged tightly into a box-shaped cutout called a mortise (B) at the tip of the bow.

The hair is held in place by a wooden, wedge-shaped plug (C) that is cut to exactly fit the space in the cutout box.

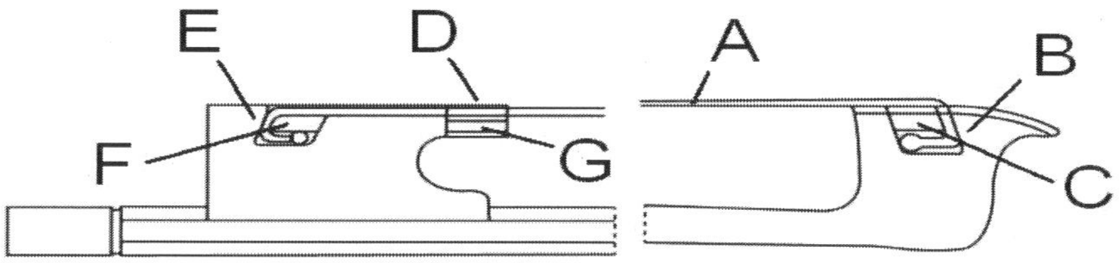

A metal band called a ferrule (D) is placed over the hair which is carefully drawn along the bow, tied at the end, and forced into another box-shaped cutout in the frog (E).

Another wooden wedge-shaped plug is placed into the box (F) to keep the hair in place.

Finally, a slide and third wooden wedge are placed between the ferrule and the frog (G) to help spread the hairs and keep them in place.

Tightening and Loosening Bow Hair — You probably learned how to tighten and loosen your bow at your first lesson. Let's take a closer look at the parts of the bow that you use when adjusting your bow hair.

This is the frog end of a bow.

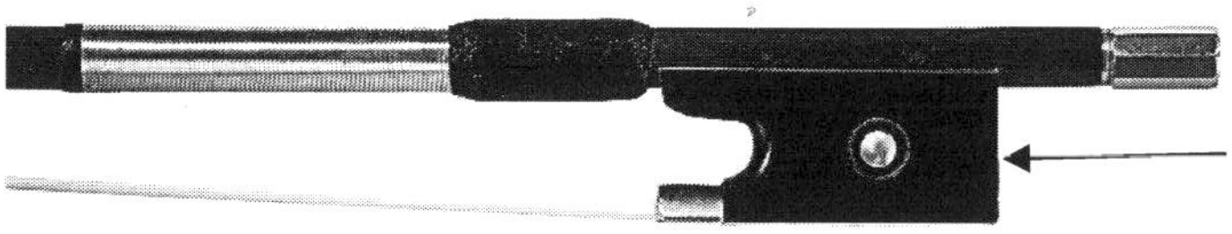

Following is a picture of the eyelet, the screw that fits into the eyelet, and a frog with the screw and eyelet together.

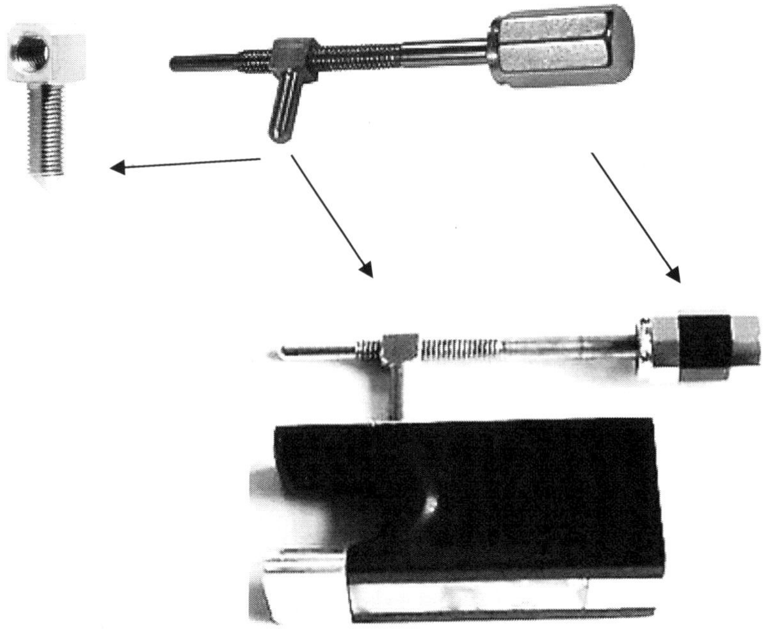

When you turn the screw, it moves in or out of the eyelet which is attached to the frog. The eyelet pulls or pushes the frog back and forth. Turning the screw to the right will pull the frog back and tighten the bow hair. Turning the screw to the left will push the frog forward and loosen the bow hair.

Lesson Six

Changing Notes

The violin has four strings that are tuned to E, A, D, and G. You are able to raise the pitch of each string by pressing the string to the fingerboard with the fingers of your left hand, as pictured below.

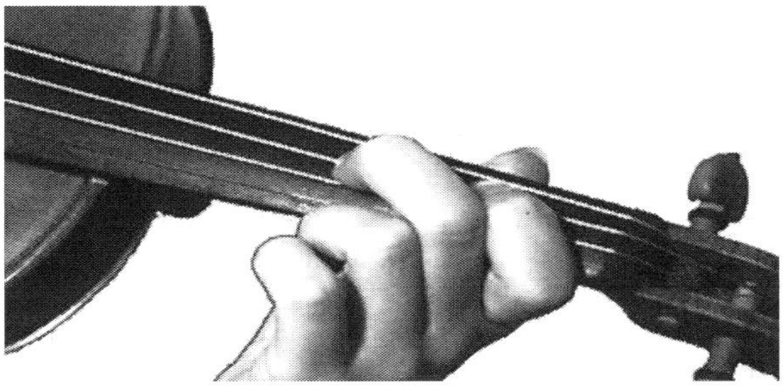

This is how it works:

As you press a finger on the string, you are shortening the part of the string that is vibrating. When plucked or bowed, shorter strings produce higher sounds. You learned in your lesson book how to finger the different notes starting with the first finger about an inch up from the bottom of the fingerboard on any string. That is called first position.

There are seven positions on the violin. Place your first, second, third, and fourth fingers on any string in the location you learned in your early violin studies.

Dr. Robin Deverich, creator of the website www.Violinonline has consented to my including the Advanced Fingering Chart 1st - 7th Positions. Using the chart below as your guide, you will see that you are playing in:

1. first position when your first finger is one whole step up from the open string.

2. second position when your first finger is where your second finger was in first position.

3. third position when your first finger is where your third finger was in first position.

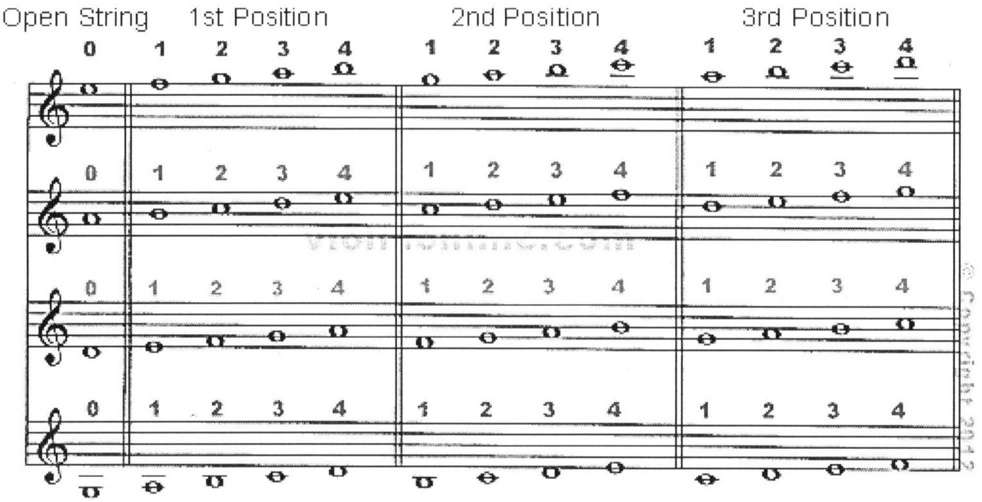

4. fourth position when your first finger is where your fourth finger was in first position.

5. fifth position when your first finger is where your second finger was in fourth position.

6. sixth position then your first finger is where your third finger was in fourth position.
7. seventh position when your first finger is where your fourth finger was in fourth position. Position Charts Compliments of violinonline.com

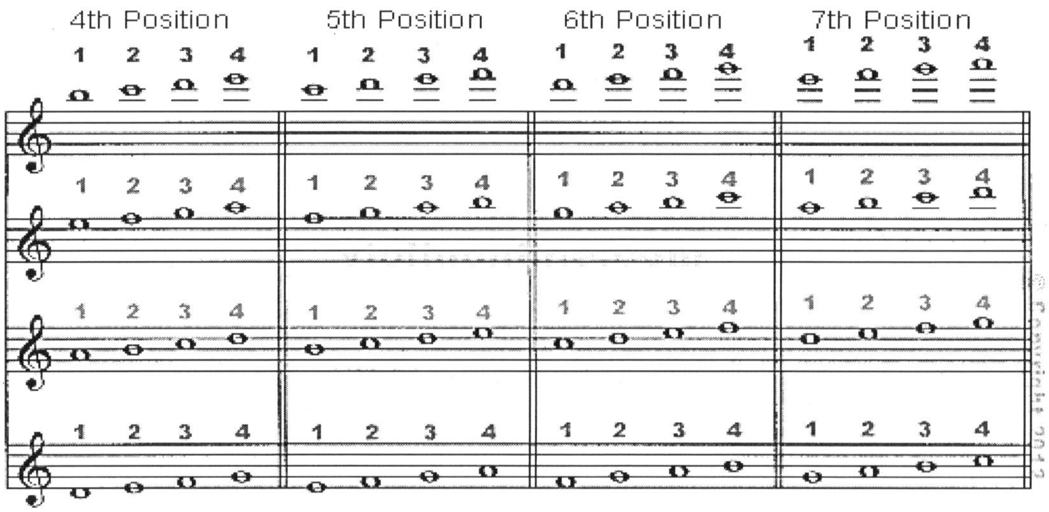

The following is a fingering chart for the notes on a violin.

To finger a note, press the string at the position noted by the dots on the fingerboard chart.

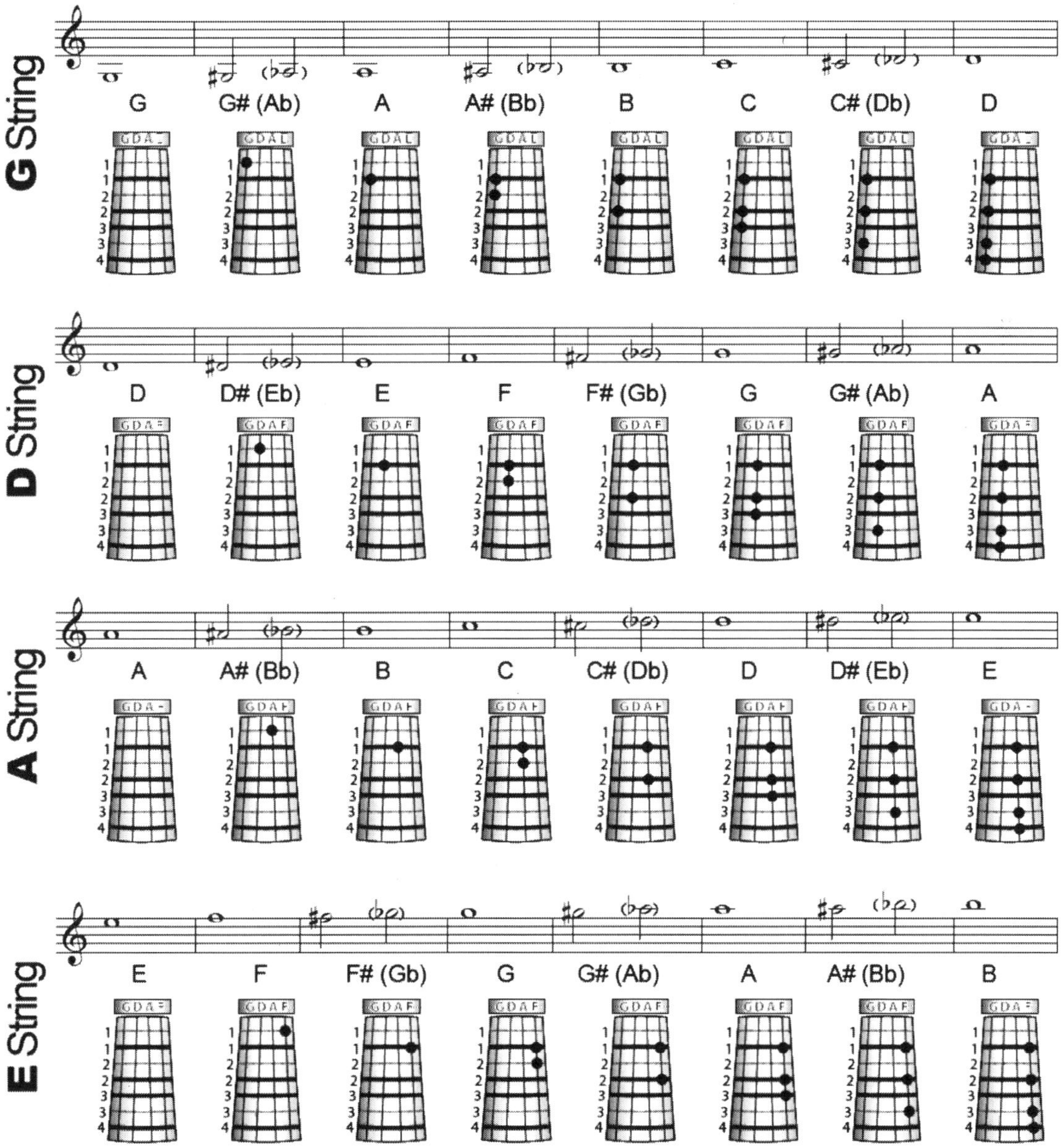

NOTES

Chapter 2

How Do I Care for My Violin Outfit?

Your violin and bow need very special care because:

1. they are made of wood that can crack or break if dropped or treated roughly,

2. the wood can be damaged by extreme heat, cold, or very damp or dry air,

3. the wood has a very fine finish that can be scratched or damaged by dirt and rosin dust.

Lesson One

Let's See How We Can Prevent These Mishaps

1. To avoid damage from dropping your violin, always place it on a safe flat surface or in its case. Do not leave it on a chair, the floor, or on a music stand.

2. Never put music or other books in your violin case. The case is made to fit the shape of your violin and does not have extra space for other items.

3. Store your violin in a place in your house where you would be comfortable...not in the attic, basement, or garage. If your violin is in its case and it is in your way, put the case under your bed.

4. Never put your violin in the trunk of a car. Keep it in the car with you where the temperature is comfortable. But! Never leave the violin in an unoccupied car. The violin can become too hot, too cold, and can be stolen.

5. The finish on your violin is probably varnish or some form of lacquer. These finishes can be scratched by a loose bow or other loose items in your case. Always

secure the bow in its case clip and keep your rosin, tuner, and other small items in the storage box at the small end of your case.

6. Wash your hands before you handle your violin. Natural hand oil or other substances on your hands can damage the surface of your instrument.

7. Follow the instruction in lesson 2 on wiping the surfaces of your instrument and strings after each use. Rosin dust left on these surfaces can damage them.

8. When traveling with your violin, keep the instrument in the same location you occupy when traveling. The luggage compartment of a bus or plane are not acceptable places for storage during travel. Keep the instrument as close to you as possible.

Lesson Two

Keeping Your Violin Outfit Clean and Properly Adjusted

After each use:

1. Wipe the surfaces of the instrument and the strings with a soft cotton cloth to remove any rosin dust, natural skin oils, and perspiration.

2. Wipe the bow stick and frog with the same cloth.

3. If your violin or bow stick begin to show signs of dirt or rosin that will not come off with the dry cloth, it is time to use violin polish. This can be bought in any music store or on line. Ask your teacher what he or she uses for the same problem.

Making Minor Adjustments

Adjusting the Bridge (Ask your teacher to help you the first time you try this.)

Each time you tune your violin, the strings move the bridge a tiny bit toward the fingerboard. To adjust your bridge:

1. Loosen the strings just a bit.

2. Place the instrument on your lap face up with the fingerboard facing away from your body.

3. Using the thumb and forefinger of each hand, grip the bridge on the middle of each side and move it back to its upright position.

4. Check the bridge feet to see if they are in perfect contact with the top of the instrument.

5. Re-tune the instrument (chapter 1).

Bridge Placement — The exact position of the bridge on your violin is very important because it carries the string's sound down to the violin's top and then throughout the entire instrument.

To check your bridge's location:

1. Look at the middle of your ***"f"*** holes and you will see a notch on each side.

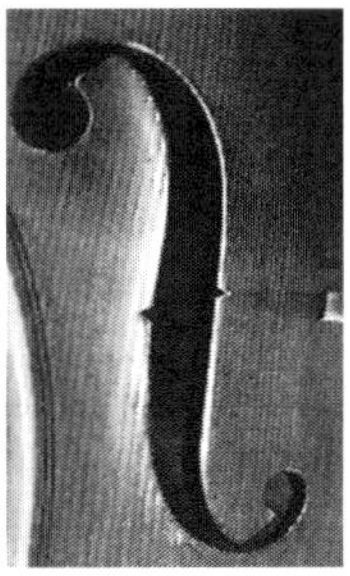

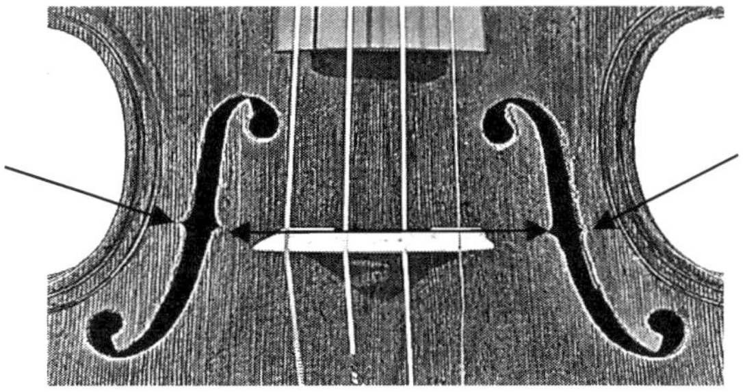

The bridge feet should be in line with the notch on the bridge side of the ***"f"*** hole.

Lesson Three

Sticking and Slipping Pegs

You learned in chapter 1 that the violin has wedge-shaped wooden pegs which are forced into holes in the peg box.

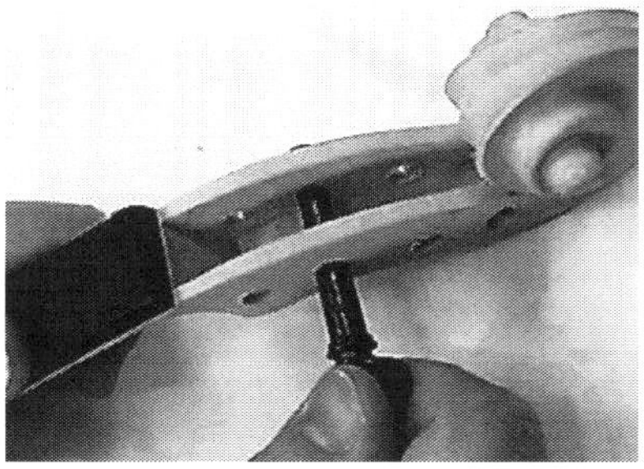

There are times when your violin pegs will either slip or get stuck. Usually, they will slip in the winter when the air is cold and dry, and they will stick in the summer when the weather is hot and humid. This happens because wood will shrink in the cold dry weather and swell in the hot humid weather.

Pegs and peg boxes are made of different kinds of wood. When the two woods shrink or swell, they can do so at different rates, so the shrinking pegs and peg holes will loosen and slip, and the swelling pegs and peg holes will tighten up and stick.

Treating this problem:

1. The old-fashioned way was to remove the pegs and apply chalk or soap to them.

2. A newer way is to remove the pegs and apply peg compound to them. Peg compound is a paste that you can buy in any music store. Follow the directions on the package.

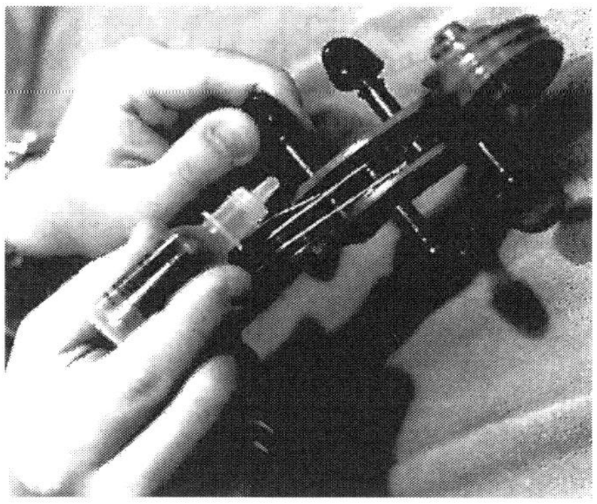

3. The newest, easiest, and best way is to apply Peg Drops (p. 36) as instructed on the package. With this product there is no need to remove the pegs.

Another cause of slipping pegs is improper wrapping of the string around the peg.

To avoid this problem:

1. Check to see if the hole that is drilled in the peg to receive a string is at the narrow end of the peg.

2. Starting from that point with the string in the hole, wind the string around the peg two turns toward the small end of the peg.

3. Then guide the string across and over the hole toward the larger side of the peg and complete the turning.

4. The turns should be lined up against each other. There should be no string buildup against the peg box wall.

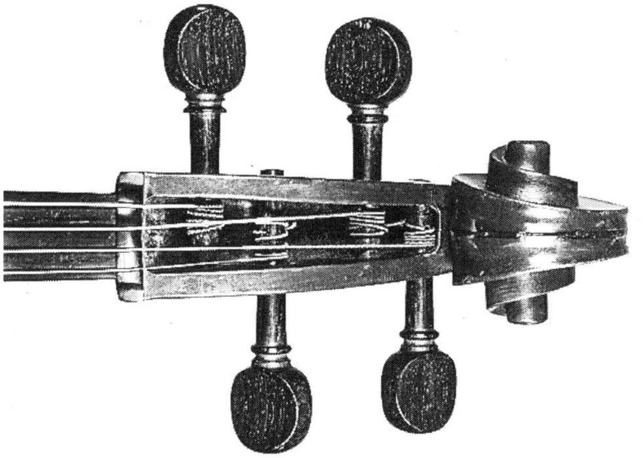

Lesson Four

Caring for Your Fine Tuners

Each time you turn the knob on your fine tuner to the right, the bottom bar gets lower.

Over time that metal bar can touch the top of your violin and scratch the surface.

The picture below shows how after many tunings, the metal bottom of the tuner can reach the top of your violin

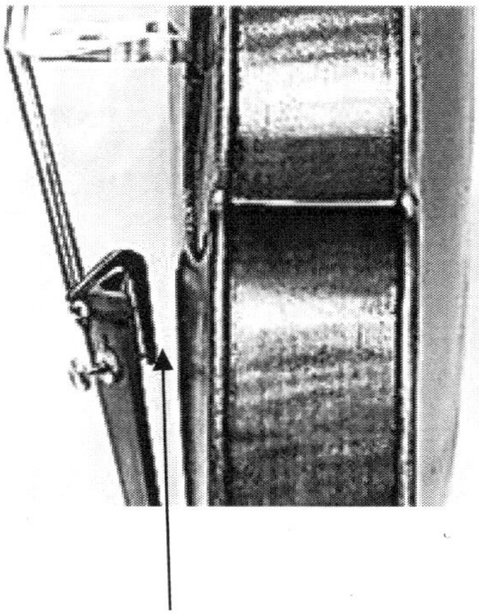

To avoid this problem, check the bottom of your tuners after tuning your violin to see when the tuner bar begins to get too close to the violin's top. When it does, turn the tuners back to the left as far as they will go. Then re-tune your violin using the peg first and then the fine tuner as needed.

Lesson Five

Bow Care

1. Always keep your bow where you keep your violin. They are both safest in their case.

2. Do not leave your bow on a music stand or on a chair. The bow can easily be knocked off the stand or, if on a chair, be sat on.

3. When preparing to use your bow, tighten your bow hair to the point where you can fit your little finger in the space between the bow stick and bow hair.

4. When your bow hair is tight, your bow stick should have a curve toward the hair.

If it does not, show it to your teacher for advice.

5. When not in use, loosen the hair on your bow.

6. Never touch the bow hair with your fingers. The natural oil from your skin will soil the hairs and the bow will not work well.

7. If a hair breaks, do not pull it off the bow. Cut it off at the frog and tip with a scissor to avoid damage to the other hairs.

Cleaning Your Bow Hair

1. To clean your bow hair, moisten a soft cloth with rubbing alcohol. With that cloth, wipe the hair in an up-and-down motion until it is clean. Do not let the alcohol touch the bow stick because the alcohol will damage the finish on the wood.

2. When the alcohol on the hair dries, gently run a comb up and down the hairs to loosen them. Then rosin your bow as usual. Ask your teacher about a product called the "Bow Hair Rejuvenation Kit" (p. 36) which is excellent for keeping your bow in good playing condition.

3. When a bow is left in a case for a long time, you may find that the hairs are falling off the stick. This is caused by tiny insects called dermestids (bow bugs). If this happens, remove the bow from the case, cut off the all the bow hair with a scissor, discard the hair and send the bow to a bow maker for rehairing.

4. Next, vacuum the case thoroughly, giving special care to the corners and edges. Then spray the case with an insecticide, and let the case remain open in a bright sunlit place for a few days.

Cleaning Your Bow Stick

1. After each use, use a soft cloth to wipe the rosin dust from your bow stick.

2. If your bow stick is caked with dry rosin, use a violin polish to clean the stick. Be extra careful to not get any violin polish on the bow hair.

Case Care

Cleaning Your Violin Case

It is important that you keep the inside and outside of your violin case clean. The insides of violin cases are lined with a special kind of material that will protect the violin from damage. That material collects lint, rosin dust, and any other small matter that enters your case.

Cases also have a rosin box inside the narrow end of the case and some cases have another box in the center of the inside. Each of these boxes has corners that collect dirt.

To care for the inside of your case, simply use a vacuum with a hose and pointed nozzle and go at it. Be sure to get into all the corners and seams in the case.

The outside of violin cases can be made of plastic, wood, or molded plastic covered with different kinds of material. Molded plastic cases can be wiped with a damp cloth and when dry, polished with a spray polish like Pledge. Fabric covered case cleaning depends on the fabric. Usually, this is canvas and can be wiped with a damp cloth (no soap) to remove any dirt or dust that has collected on the case cover.

Violins and bows can last hundreds of years if they are properly cared for. The process is not hard to do, nor does it take much time. Make a habit of going through the above listed procedures on a regular basis and your violin might also be here a few hundred years from now.

Lesson Six

Adjustments

Strings

The strings on your violin rest on the violin's nut (A), bridge (B), and tailpiece (C) (see arrows). Over time, those three areas can wear down. If you see string wear, or wear on the slots where the string meets the nut, bridge, or tailpiece, ask your teacher's advice on how to deal with the problem.

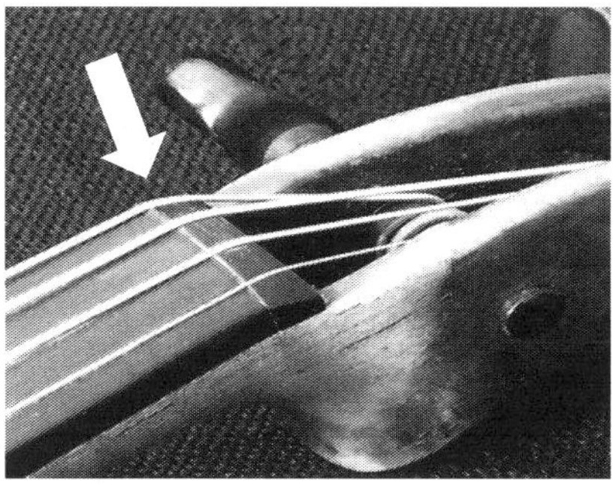

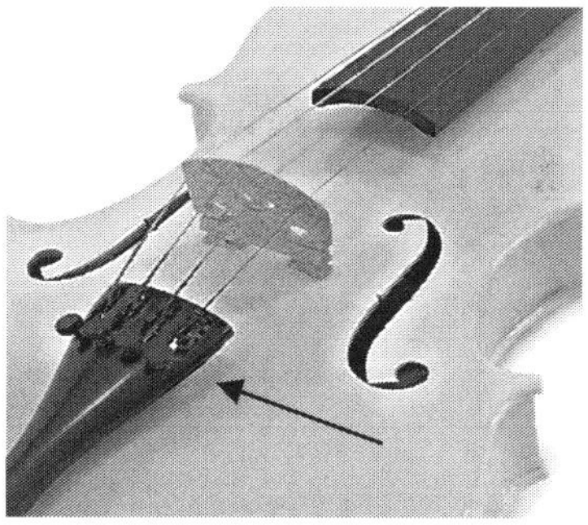

(A) Nut **(B) Bridge** **(C) Tailpiece**

If the string is wearing out, simply replace it. If one of those three parts is showing wear, you will need a luthier (violin maker) to replace the nut and the bridge. You can replace the tailpiece with your teacher's help.

Summary — Properly caring for your violin, bow, and case will give them a long life and allow them to serve you in the best way possible. These three items are the tools that you will use to make music. A good student with good equipment will make good music.

NOTES

Chapter 3

How Should I Plan My Practice Sessions?

I am sure you have heard that "practice makes perfect". Well, indeed, practice can make perfect but only if you practice with understanding, and the patience and the will to "get it right". Playing an exercise or musical selection many times over will not make it better unless you understand how the piece should sound and know what to do to make it sound that way. Playing a piece incorrectly over and over can result in your learning to play it wrong really well. These are some suggestions that will help you get the best results from your violin practice period:

1. Select a place in your home where you will be able to practice without disturbing your family and where their daily life will not distract you from your work.

2. Pick a practice time that will fit into your daily study schedule comfortably. Try to use that same time each day for your violin studies.

3. Set a long-term general goal. In what ways do you want to improve your playing? Think of bowing, intonation, phrasing, dexterity (moving your fingers fast), and making beautiful music beautifully.

4. Have a plan for each practice period. What part of your long-term goal do you want to accomplish in each period?

5. How long and how often should you practice? Daily practice is best. However, how long you practice should vary with your short-term goal. Shorter periods of daily practice more often produce better results than less frequent long sessions.

6. After you have planned your goal and begun to practice, you will decide on the amount of time and how often practice will be necessary to achieve each target.

7. Discuss your plans with your teacher, who will be able to help you make the plan and reach your goal. The amount of time you spend practicing is not as important as is what you accomplish during your practice period.

8. Equipment – It is important that you have all the equipment necessary to have a successful practice period. Your equipment should include a music stand, metronome, chair if you plan to sit, comfortable chin rest, shoulder rest, rosin, cleaning cloth, and anything else that you feel you need to be comfortable.

The Process

1. Begin your practice period with a careful tuning of your violin. Use whatever apps or tuning device you feel will be best for you.

2. Warm up starting with some simple scales in first position using quarter notes. Play slowly and listen. Are you playing in tune?

3. After the quarter note scales, add rhythmic patterns of your own creation to those same scales. Listen carefully to intonation as you play. Playing in tune is a must for any violinist.

4. As you advance, you can expand the warmup material to include exercises and any other music you enjoy playing.

5. Follow your warm up with playing a tune that you like. Enjoy the music.

6. Improvisation is fun. Make up your own tune or try to play a tune "by ear". No need for printed music here.

7. Now start practicing the material your teacher assigned at your last lesson.

Follow the instructions carefully. Listen to yourself, sing the music before you play it, feel the rhythm and be sure you are playing in tune.

8. Record yourself on your iPhone as you play. Then listen to the recording and be very critical of your intonation, phrasing, and general musicianship.

9. Did you like what you heard? If your answer is yes – great! If it is no, think of what you did not like. Figure out how you can make it better. Then, make it better. Check again to be sure you are playing in tune, using proper phrasing, and proper bowing. Are you keeping a proper playing position?

Apps and Your iPhone

Using your iPhone or computer, you can search for "Apps for violin practice and tuning". You will find many that are free and will help you tune and practice better. Some sites also have free music that you can print. Others show playing techniques and play-a-long sessions where you join in with others to play violin music. Use the same search on YouTube and you will find many sites that you will enjoy watching while learning about playing your violin.

The following are just a few of the many apps that you can find on your iPhone or computer.

Best Violin App for iPhone
Violin Notes App
Play Along Violin App
Play Along Violin App Android

Free Violin Music
Violin App for Android
Violin Tuner App
Free Online Violin Tuner Metronome

NOTES

Chapter 4

What Items (Accessories) Will I Need to Help Me Play My Violin?

An accessory is something that will help you use your violin but is not part of a basic violin outfit. The descriptions and pictures of accessories below are just some of these items. You can find hundreds more on Google.

Rosin — Rosin, made from tree sap (resin), is used to make the hair on your violin bow sticky. This makes the hair grip the violin string as you bow to produce sound.

Rosin comes in shades of amber (yellow), from light to dark. Prices range from 99 cents to $35. and in some "very special" cases even more. If you are a beginning student, it would be best to start with the least expensive rosin available. It will work fine until either your teacher recommends a change, or you feel you need something different. Be sure to use "violin rosin" as rosin for other instruments will be too sticky for use on your violin bow.

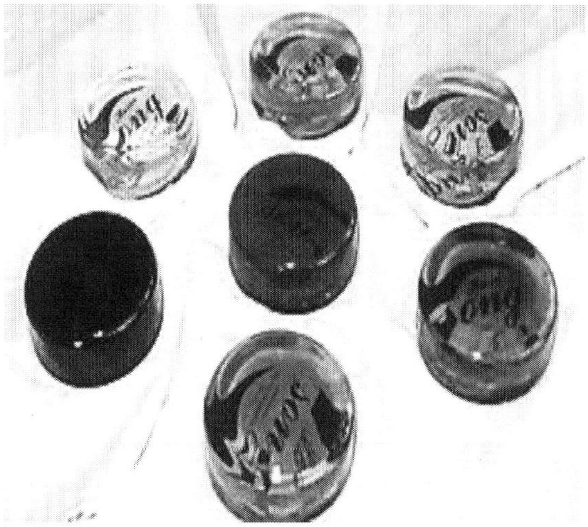

Rosin can have different degrees of hardness and color. Hard rosin, usually light amber in color, gives a dry powdery result. Its gripping power is lighter and best for the violin.

Soft rosin, darker in color, has a stickier texture and provides increased gripping power for the bow hair. This greater gripping power will produce a stronger sound.

Tuning Forks — The tuning fork is the most basic device used to hear a pitch. Tuning forks are U-shaped, and made of metal with a handle at the base of the U.

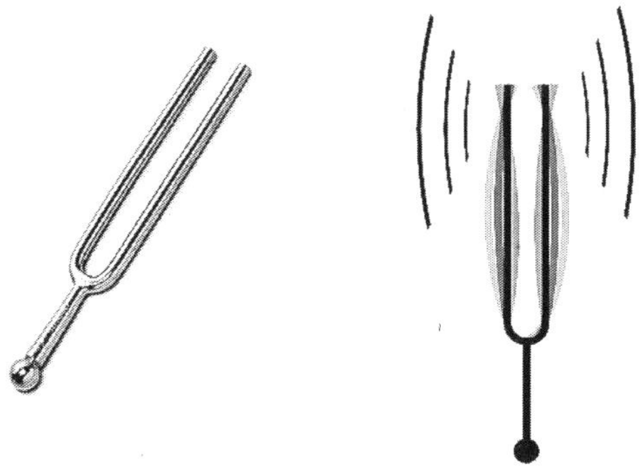

Hold a tuning fork by the handle and strike the tines (prongs) on a hard surface. The tines will vibrate. Then touch the stem to a hard surface and you will hear the tone (pitch) caused by the vibrations. You can get a tuning fork for any pitch, but A440 (440 vibrations per second) is the pitch A you would use to tune your violin A string.

Pitch Pipes — A pitch pipe is a necessary accessory for any violin player. The simplest pitch pipe is made with four small pipes joined together. Each pipe is tuned to match the pitch of one string on your violin. The pitches from low to high for the violin are G, D, A, and E. You blow gently into the correct pipe to hear the pitch you need to tune a string.

A chromatic pitch pipe is round and has a marked opening for every pitch including the sharps and flats (chromatics) in the scale. The notes start at C and progress in half steps up to the next C in the scale. You can pick any note, slide the white marker to that note's position on the pitch pipe, blow into that hole, and hear the pitch you choose.

Electronic Tuners —There are two kinds of electronic tuners. The simpler type produces the four pitches of the open strings for your violin. Other models have all the notes. You select the pitch needed, press the correct button, and you hear the pitch.

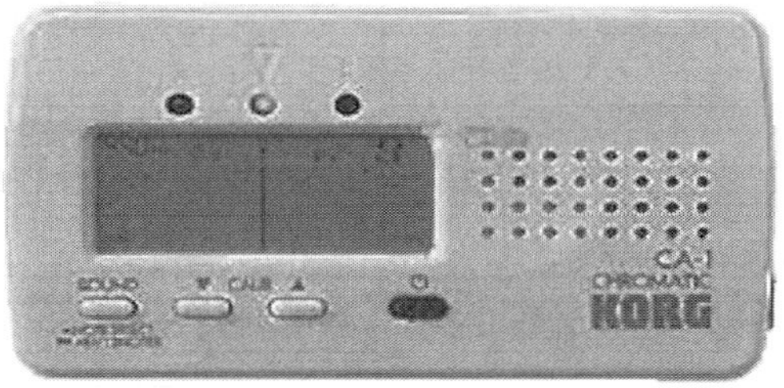

A more advanced type of tuner has a screen which shows an image of the pitch being sounded. When you bow or pluck a string, a needle on a screen will tell you if the sound is higher, lower, or exactly on the pitch you want. You can then tune the string up or down until the correct pitch is reached.

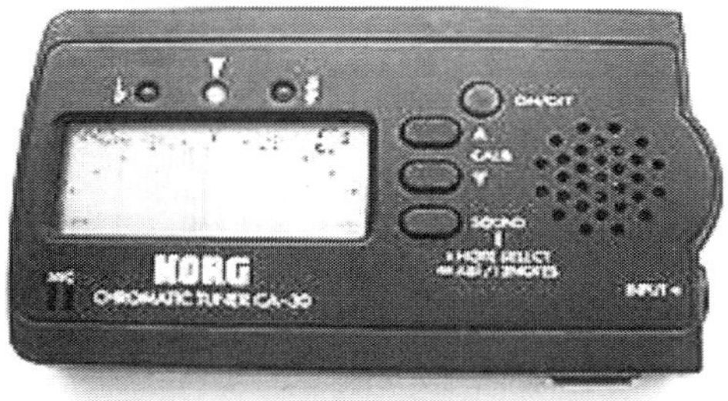

Apps or Applications — Apps and websites on tuning can be found on your iPhone, iPad, and computer. If you use one of these, try not to be distracted by using your practice time on trying the technology. Amazon.com shows five pages, each with about fifteen different tuners for a total of seventy-five tuners of all kinds now on the market.

Fine Tuners — Fine tuners are attached to the tailpiece or the string of a violin and are available in different forms. The Suzuki model fine tuners are independent tuners that are attached directly to a string.

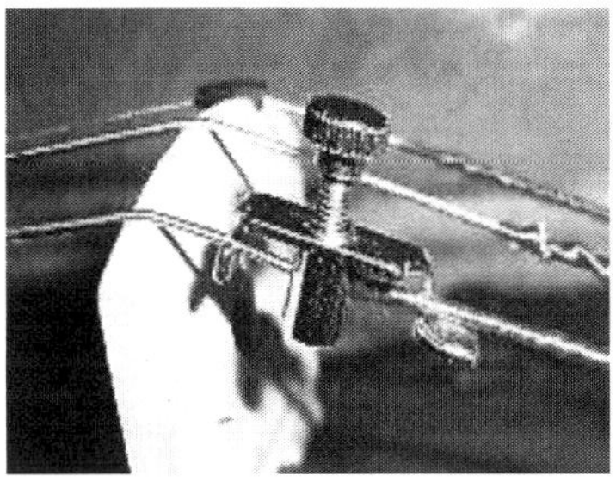

Another style fine tuner attaches to the tailpiece, and the string is then connected directly to the fine tuner.

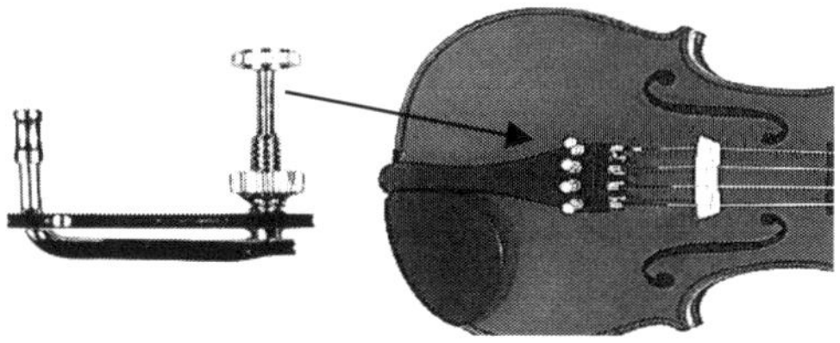

There are also tuners that are part of the tailpiece. With this arrangement the string is attached to the fine tuner instead of directly to the tailpiece.

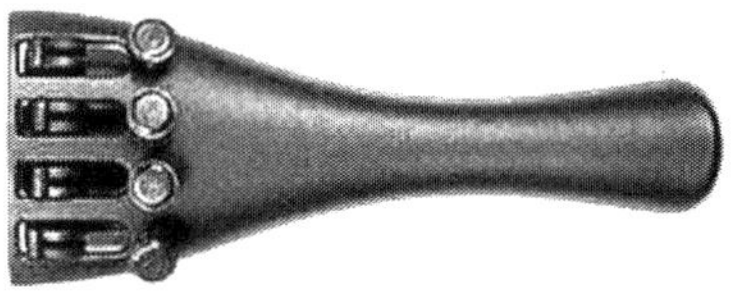

Peg Treatment — Peg compound is a heavy paste that you put on the pegs to stop them from sticking or slipping.

Peg Drops — This is a liquid treatment. Put one drop on the peg at the two points where it comes in contact with the peg box and then slide the peg back into place.

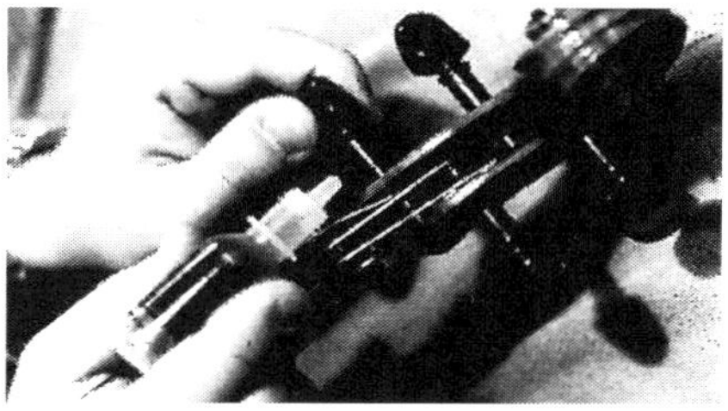

Bow Hair Rejuvenation Kit — This kit is used to remove rosin buildup and dirt from your bow hair.

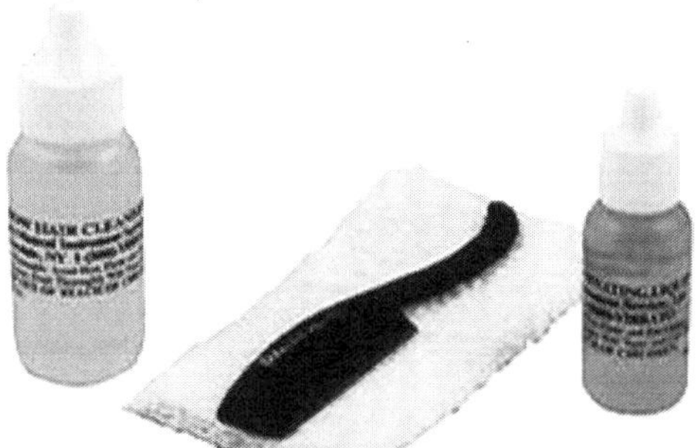

Strings — As you progress in your studies, you will want to learn more about the different kinds of violin strings and how they can improve the sound of your violin. A search on Google shows fifty-seven different brands of violin strings. These strings can be made of gut, steel, perlon (plastic fiber), nylon, silk, chromium/steel, and gold. Each type of string produces a different sound and can change the tone quality of your violin.

Steel or Steel Core strings are strongest, produce the brightest sound, stay in tune longer, and are best for use by beginning players.

Gut Strings produce a more mellow sound, but they react to changes in temperature and humidity. This can cause problems with keeping your violin in tune. Gut strings tend to break more easily than steel strings.

Gut Core strings are gut strings which are wound with silver or aluminum. These produce a fuller sound than plain gut and are stronger.

Synthetic Core strings are made with nylon or another manmade material as a core. These strings are stronger than gut, do not react greatly to temperature and humidity changes, and stay in tune longer.

Strings are made with either a ball end, loop end, or knot end which is connected to the tailpiece. The loop and ball ends are usually found on most strings whereas the knot end is used for gut strings without windings.

Chin Rests — There is probably a model chin rest to meet every violin player's needs. A new player should begin by using the chin rest that comes with the instrument. If that chin rest is not comfortable, visit a music store that specializes in violins and try all the chin rests available. They come in different sizes and shapes and can place your chin at any point on the instrument from the far left to the center over the tailpiece.

Chin rests are made of Bakelite, ebony, rosewood, assorted plastics, and practically any other specialty material. Choose the shape and material that suits your comfort and pocketbook best. The material from which a chin rest is made is not important. Below are four different shaped chinrests.

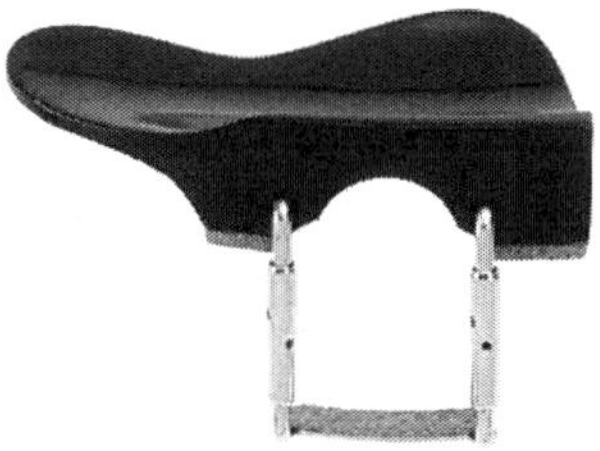

Chin Rest Pads — Chin rest pads are items for your comfort. They are available as corduroy pockets that slip over your chin rest, gel-filled pads that stick on to the chin rest, and felt pads that attach with Velcro. Below are four different kinds of chin rest pads.

Gel Rest

Chin Chum

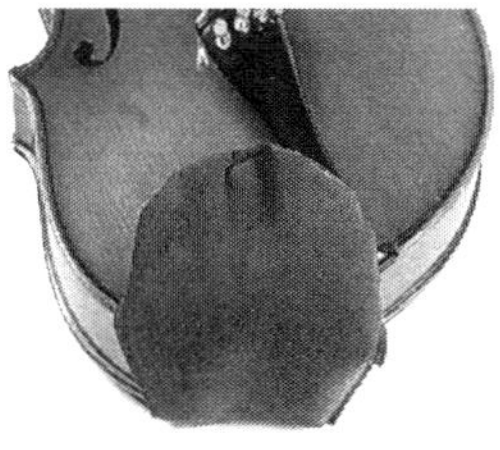

Chin Cozy

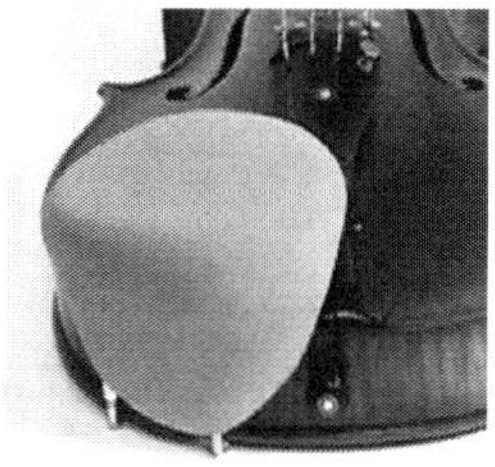

Strad Pad

Shoulder Rests — If you find it hard to hold your violin with your chin and shoulder, you may try a shoulder rest. It will help you keep the proper playing position by supporting the instrument. That support also leaves your left hand free to shift positions.

Some of the brand names are Kun, Viva La Musica, Wolf, Resonans, Bonmusica, Mach One, Everest, Stowmaster, and Pede Elegante. These all offer their versions of the same basic model and are available in many sizes.

Kun Shoulder Rest can be adjusted in both height and width.

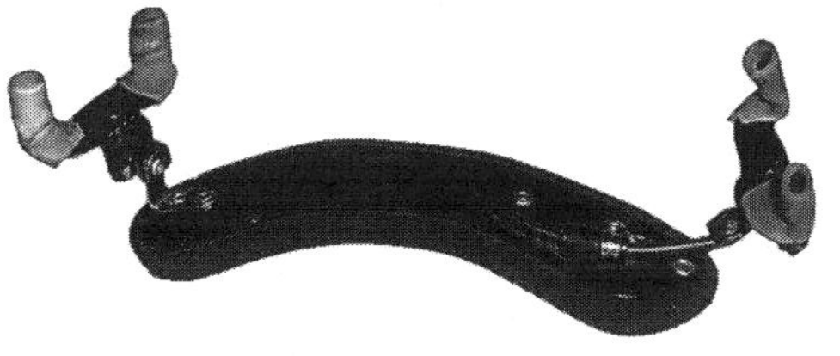

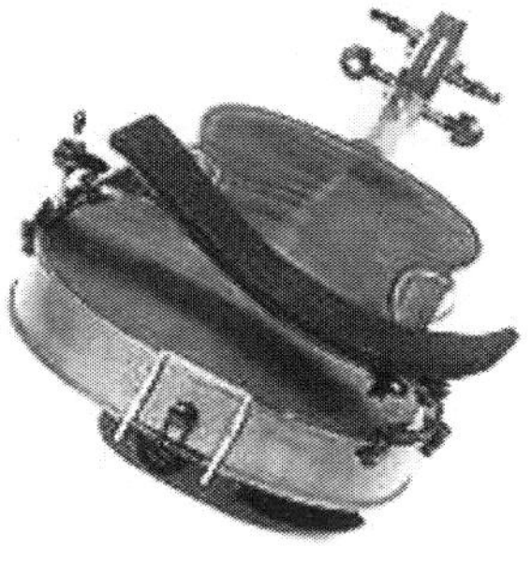

Play-On-Air is an inflatable pillow that comes in five different sizes. You fill it with air by blowing into a tube much like that used on a beach ball.

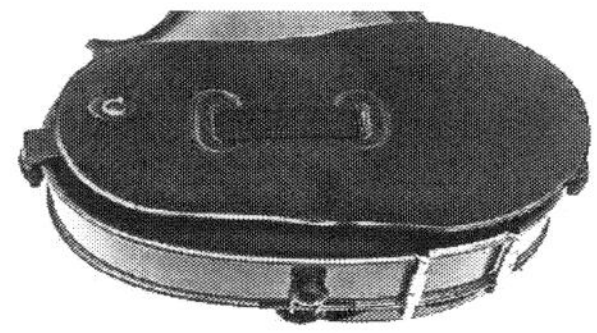

Poehland is one of the older shoulder rest models. It is a half-circular, fabric-covered firm pad attached to the end button of a violin by a leather strip and the lower bout edge of the violin body by a combination of a leather strip and a rubber band.

Zaret shoulder rest is a very inexpensive foam pad made for use on a violin.

Mutes — A mute changes the tone quality and volume of a violin's sound. Mutes can be made of wood with three or four prongs, a rubber disk with two openings for the strings, or wire shape with a plastic arch. Below are three examples of mutes.

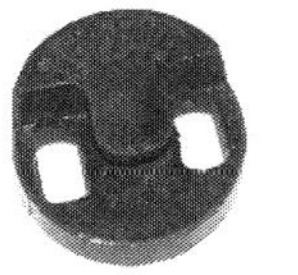

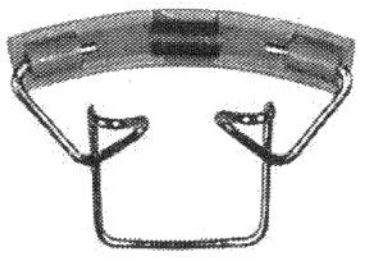

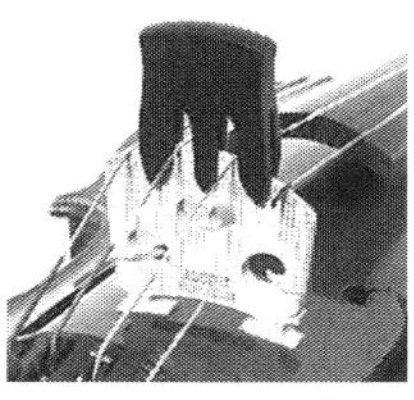

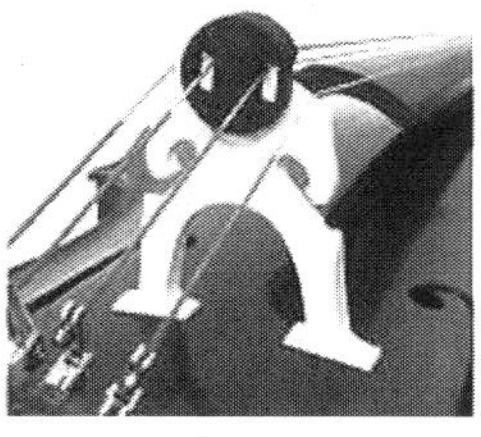

Violin Cases — Violin cases can be violin shaped, oblong, or halfmoon shaped. The cases can be made of wood, plastic, or any other combination of material that can be formed into the needed shape.

Shaped cases made of molded plastic are usually the least expensive and best for beginning students. Better quality shaped cases can be made of wood or pressed material that is covered with fabric. Below is a molded plastic case.

Oblong cases can be made of hard thermo-plastic, fiberglass, or a fabric covered wood. They are larger than the shaped case and include a pocket built onto the outside fabric cover that can be used to carry music and other violin accessories. Below are two oblong cases.

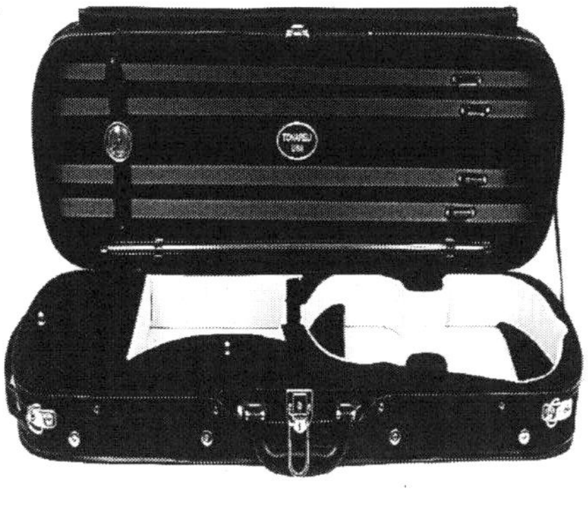

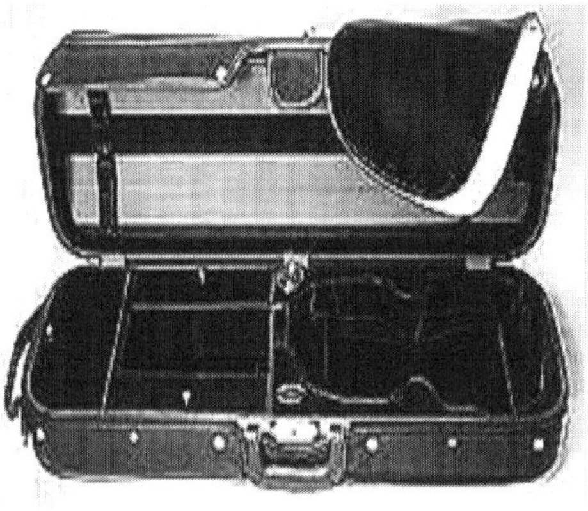

The insides of these cases can have a felt covering with a small rosin box at the scroll end or a very beautiful padding with a blanket for the violin, four satin-lined brackets for four bows, tubes to carry extra strings, a large box for rosin, a shoulder rest, tuning device, and whatever else you wish to carry.

Both the shaped and oblong upgraded cases can also include a suspension system where the violin is suspended so that the body and bridge do not come in contact with any part of the case.

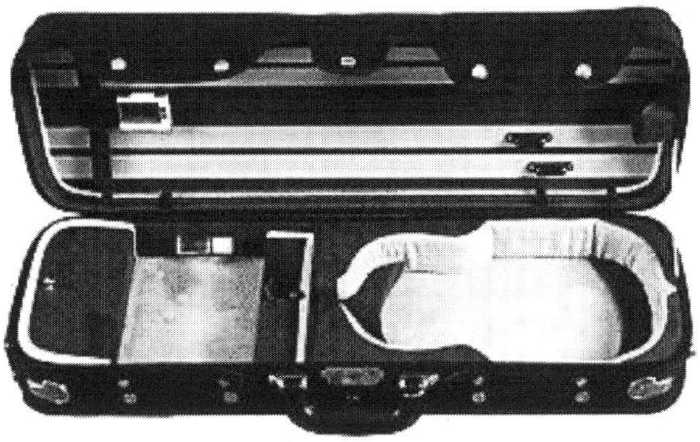

Half-moon shaped cases have all the features of the oblong case above but within a half-moon shape.

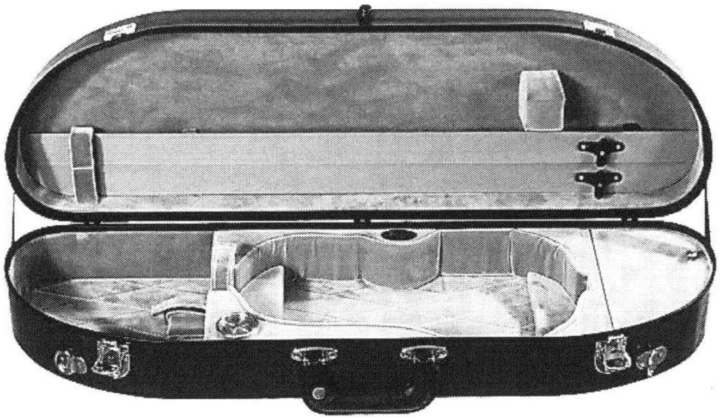

Hygrometers — A hygrometer measures the level of humidity in a violin case. If a hygrometer shows a dry climate, you will need to place a humidifier in the case. Below are two of many kinds of hygrometers.

Digital **Analog**

Humidifiers — A Dampit case humidifier is a perforated rubber tube filled with absorbent material that holds water. When your violin is not in use, insert the Dampit tube soaked in water into the body of the instrument through the F hole. Remove the Dampit when you use the instrument. A humidity-measuring color chart that shows the humidity level is included with the Dampit kit.

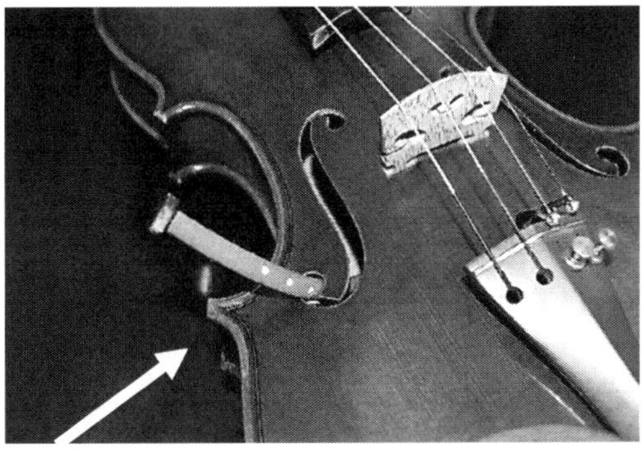

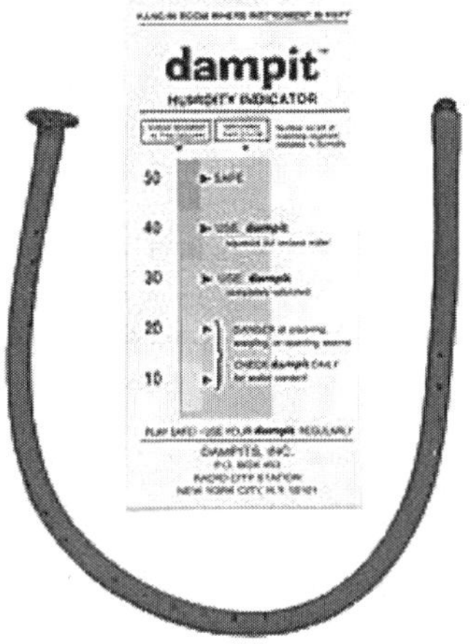

Search "violin case humidifiers" on Google Images and you will find more of these products.

Music Stands — Music stands are made in three designs. There are stands that fold, those that are rigid or non-folding, and tabletop stands.

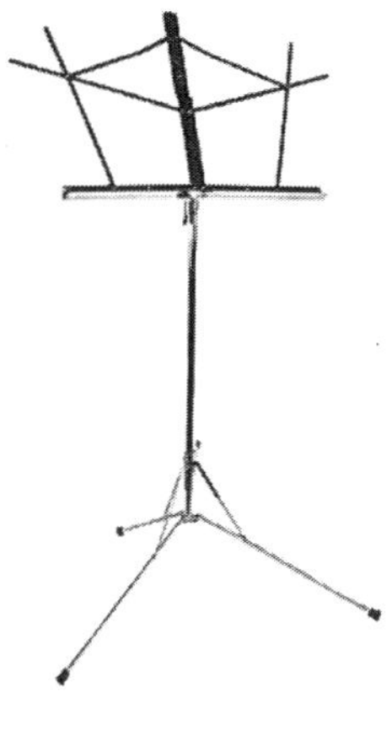

A folding stand or sheet music stand is very useful for a beginning student. It is lightweight, totally portable, and very inexpensive. Folding stands can also be purchased with a carrying case for even more convenient portability. These stands can easily be knocked over and the lightweight parts can be bent out of shape.

A rigid design stand, sometimes referred to as concert, stage, or orchestra music stand, is not easy to carry, is quite heavy, and made to be used in one place. It is more expensive than the folding stand but is very stable, able to hold a large amount of music, and is very strong. A rigid stand can cost from two to four times that of a folding stand.

A tabletop stand is small, does not have legs, is lightweight and inexpensive. It can be placed on any stable surface and allows complete flexibility. Below are three models of table top stands: the first a decorative model, the second a folding design, and the third a concert style.

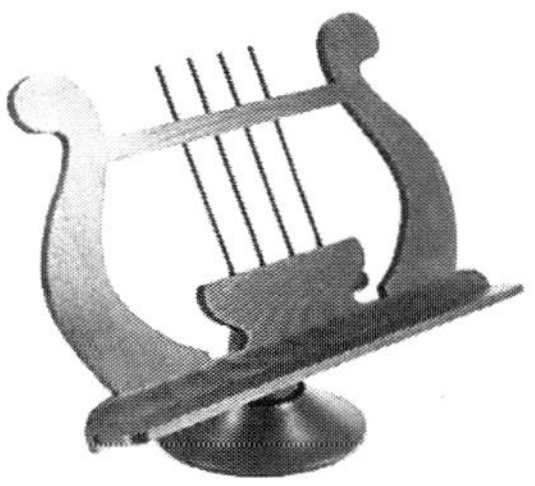

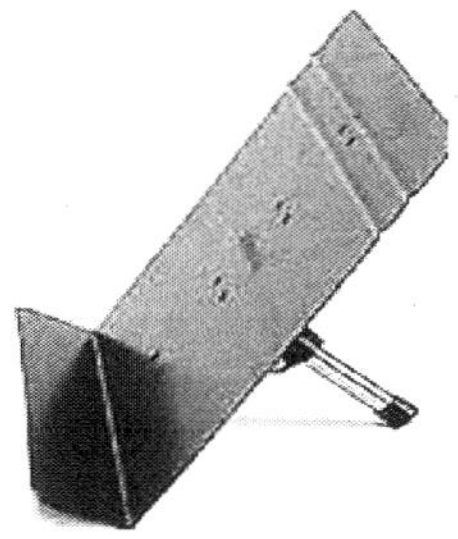

Summary This chapter showed some accessories that can make your violin study easier. To see more accessories for your violin, google "violin accessories" and you might spend the day looking through the results.

NOTES

Chapter 5

How Are Violins Made?

Understanding how your violin is made helps you better understand how it works and how to play it. Violins can be custom made, handmade, or factory made.

Custom Made means handmade by a luthier (violin maker) for a certain customer. This how it is done:

1. The luthier chooses the wood to be used. These woods may come from different parts of the world because the same kind of wood grown in unlike climates will develop differently.
   A. Maple wood is used for the back, sides, and neck of a violin.
   B. Spruce wood is used to make the top of a violin.
   C. Ebony or rosewood is used for the fingerboard, pegs, purfling, and trim.

Other kinds of woods and manmade products such as plastic and metal can be used as substitutes; however, maple, spruce, rosewood, and ebony have been found to be the best materials for making a good violin.

2. The next step in the process is designing the instrument. Usually, a copy of the designs of the masters such as Stradivari, Guarneri, and Amati are used as a start. The luthier then can adjust the design to suit his or her needs.

3. When the wood and design patterns are decided upon, the luthier carves, shapes, and molds the violin parts to fit the design selected.

4. Now the luthier fits the instrument with pegs, tailpiece, bridge, strings, and a chinrest.

5. The violin is then assembled, stained, varnished, and hand rubbed.

Handmade violins can be made by more than one luthier within a shop. Each part of a violin is made by a luthier who specialize in making that part. The handmade parts are then assembled by still another maker and setup by yet another. The instrument is still handmade but by more than one pair of hands.

Factory Made violins are made of parts carved by computer-guided woodworking machines. The parts are put together by hand.

The Process

Step 1 – Establishing the Pattern — The luthier will decide on the size and shape of the violin to be made. Usually it will be a copy of one of the great masters such as Stradivari, Amati, or any of the other master violin makers you will read about in chapter 6.

Step 2 – Selecting the Materials — The major parts of the violin will be made of spruce for the top, maple for the sides, back, and neck, and ebony or rosewood for the fingerboard, pegs, and trim. Small inner parts called blocks and linings are often made of willow.

Definition: The "grain" is the pattern or shape of the fibers you see in a piece of wood.

A violin made from wood with an even grain will produce a better sound. If the luthier makes a one-piece top or back, the grain will spread out as it goes across the piece. If a triangle cut described below is used, the piece of wood is taken from a smaller section of the tree and the grain will be closer.

Step 3 – Cutting the Wood — There are two ways wood can be cut to make the top and back (plates) of a violin. For a two-piece top or back:
1. a V- shaped block is cut out of a slice of a tree stump.

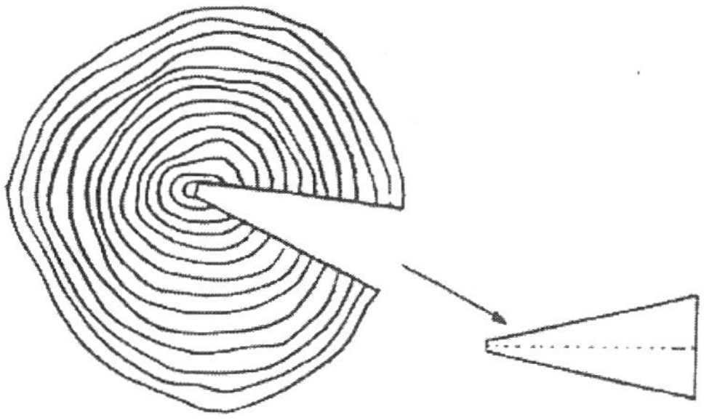

2. The V-shape is cut down its center to form two separate triangular pieces.

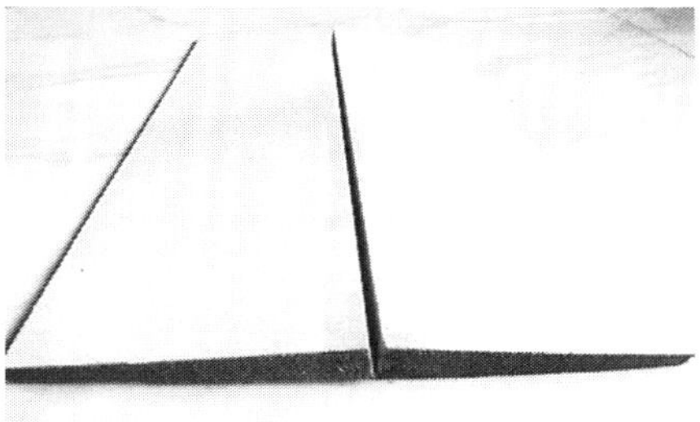

Step 4 – Joining the Cuts — The two pieces are joined together "book matched" with hide glue, a glue that can be melted with warm water.

The matched pieces of the two-piece top or back are placed in a clamp to dry. When the glue is dry, the matched pieces will form one piece. Below are pictures of wood being "book matched", glued together, and drying in a clamp.

When the two pieces that have become one are removed from the clamp, an outline of a violin's back is traced on to that piece, and the wood is cut following the outline. The final result is a violin with a two piece back shown below.

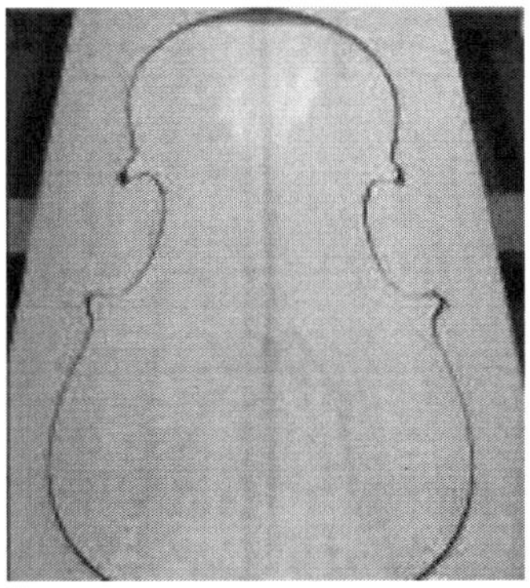
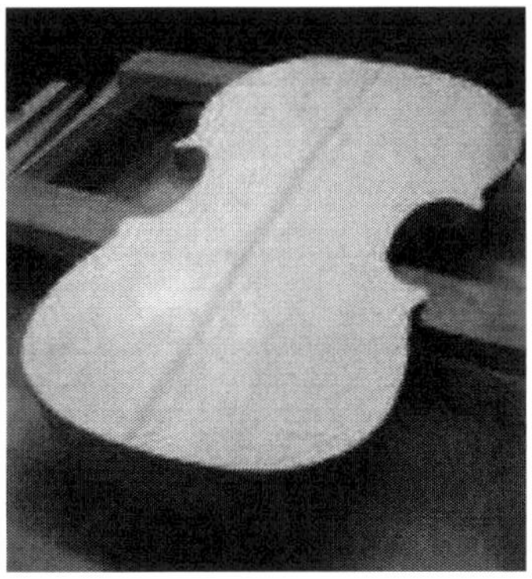
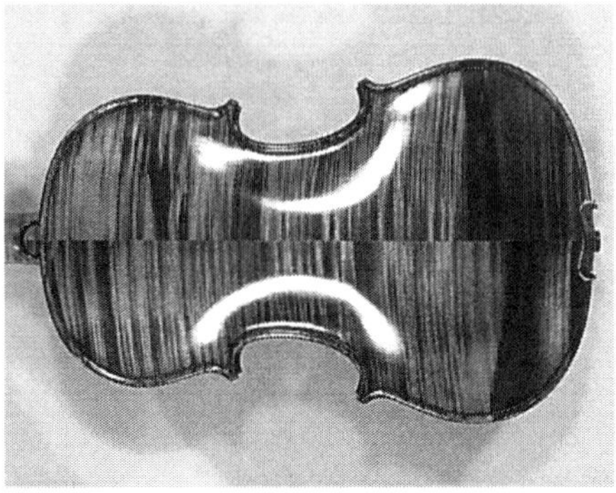

If the luthier decides on a one-piece top or back:

1. A layer of wood large enough to make an entire back or top is cut from a tree stump.

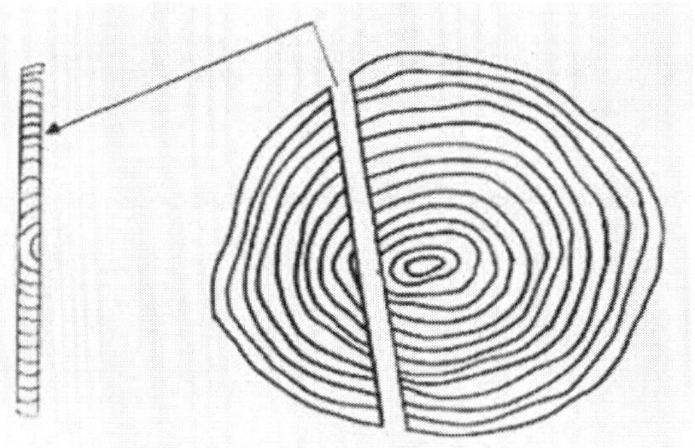

2. That slice of wood is used to make a top or back without a seam in the middle.

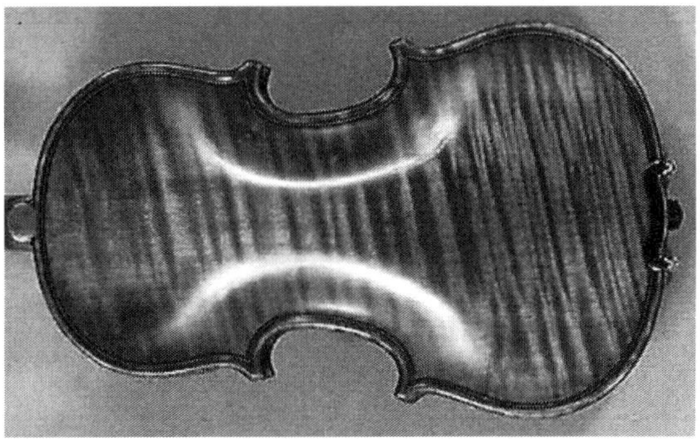

Definition: The term "bout" is used to identify the three sections of a violin body. The upper third is called the upper bout, the middle section is called the C bout, and the lower third is called the lower bout.

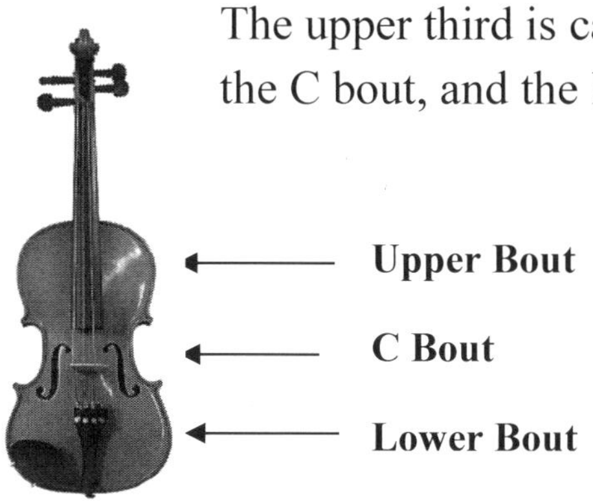

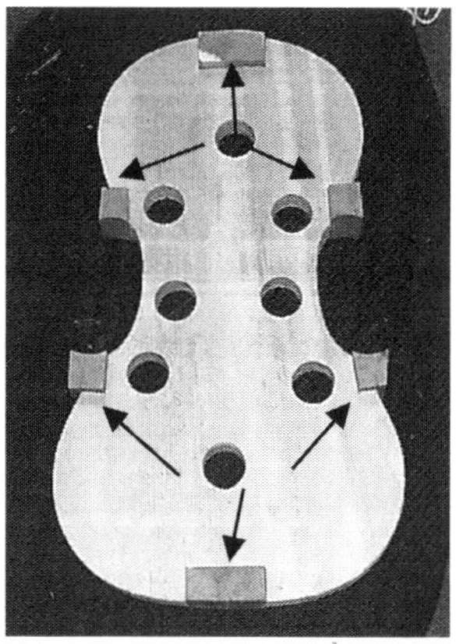

Step 5 – The Mold — A mold is a violin-shaped wooden form which the luthier uses as a base for building the first parts of a violin.

The luthier will place six wooden blocks (see arrows) on the mold to act as anchors for the instrument's sides or ribs. One (corner) block is placed in each of the four corners of the C bouts and a fifth and sixth (end) block are placed at the upper and lower end of the mold.

Step 6 – The Ribs — The ribs (sides) of a violin are thin strips of maple wood. To create the ribs, the luthier wets thin wood strips to make them bend more easily. He or she then heats and bends the strips to shape and glues them onto the six corner blocks shown above.

Step 7 - The Linings — After the ribs have been glued to the blocks and the glue is dry, thin strips of wood called linings are glued inside the edge of the ribs. The linings support the ribs after they are removed from the mold.

Step 8 – Carving the Plates — In step 4, "joining the cuts", the top and back were rough cut. These now must be carved into the shapes that will produce the best possible sound.

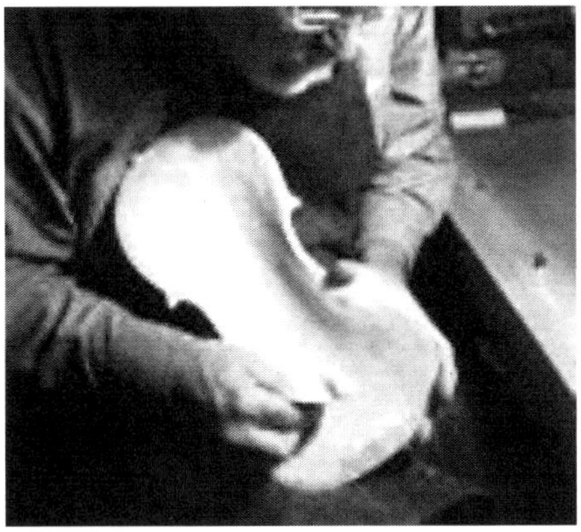
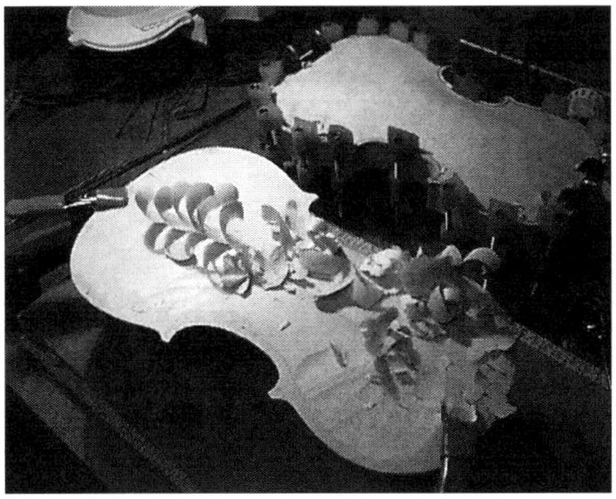

Step 9 – Purfling — Purfling is a thin, double strip of wood that is set into the edge of the top and back of a violin. Purfling strengthens the edges of the violin and controls the vibrations that are traveling through the wood.

The picture below shows a luthier marking a groove (A), cutting a groove (B), and the finished product with the purfling installed (C).

A **B** **C**

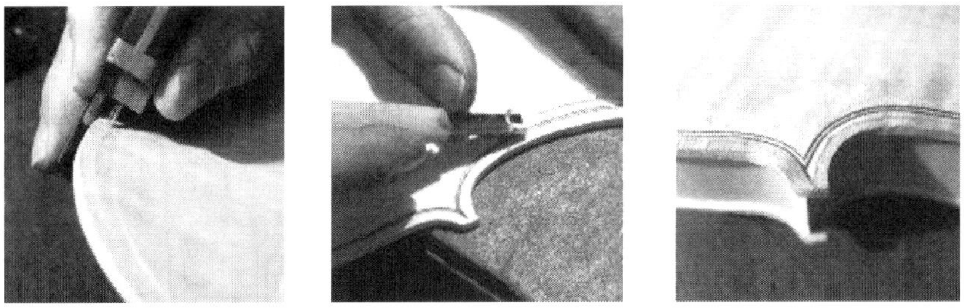

Step 10 – Tuning the Plates — It is now time for the luthier to carve the wood of the top and back of the violin so that they will vibrate to produce the best sound for that instrument. There are two ways for him or her to decide on how much wood to remove from the two plates and from where.

Originally it was done by the luthier tapping the plate and listening to the sound the tapping produces. Using the tapping method, the luthier gently holds a plate between the thumb and forefinger and with the other hand taps on the plate in different places. This will produce "tap-tones" which are actual pitches that will show the experienced luthier how much wood should be shaved from different areas of the plate to get the best sound.

In 1787 Ernest Chladni, known as the father of acoustics (the study of sound), discovered that if you run a bow along the edge of a plate (violin top or back) held tightly in a clamp and sprinkled with glitter, the plate will vibrate, and the glitter will move into certain patterns. The pattern of the glitter will show where vibration occurs and where to carve and not to carve away some more wood. These patterns were called Chladni patterns. Below are two examples of Chladni patterns.

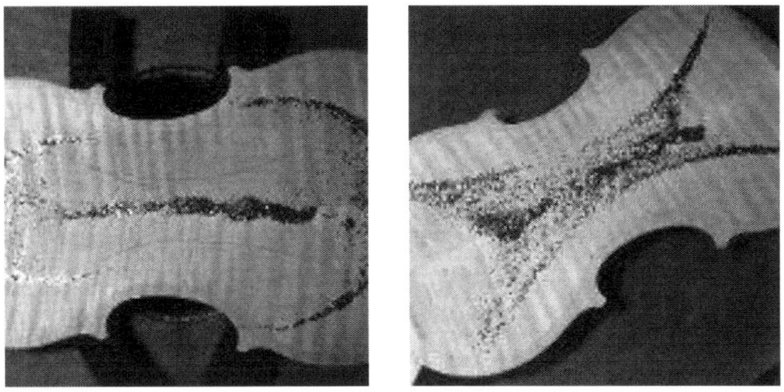

Step 11 – *"f"* Holes — The shape and size of the *"f"* holes or sound holes on a violin are important parts of the sound producing system. A luthier can greatly improve a violin's sound by the way the *"f"* holes are cut. If the size, shape, and distance of the holes from each other are properly designed, the sound of the violin will be greatly improved. *"f"* holes must be at least large enough to allow a sound post to pass through later in the making process.

To make the *"f"* holes, the luthier marks the shape on the violin's top plate, drills guide holes in places that will outline the pattern of the hole, and then uses a jeweler's saw to make the cuts. The job is then finished with a series of very sharp knives.

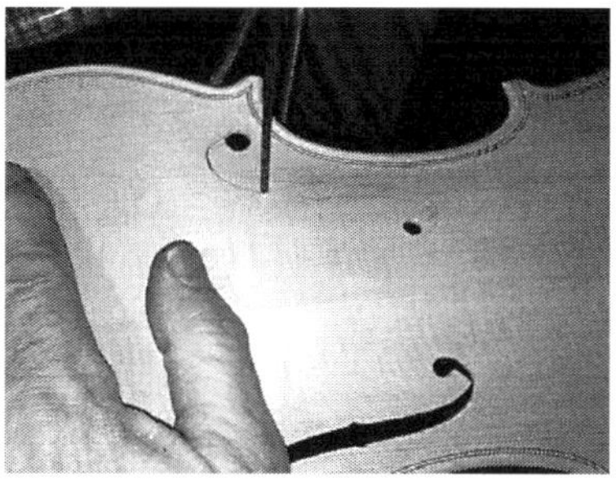

Step 12 - The Bass Bar — As you read in chapter 1, the bass bar is a strip of wood attached to the underside of the top plate. This strip strengthens the plate while spreading the lower pitches throughout that area.

The bass bar is then glued in place.

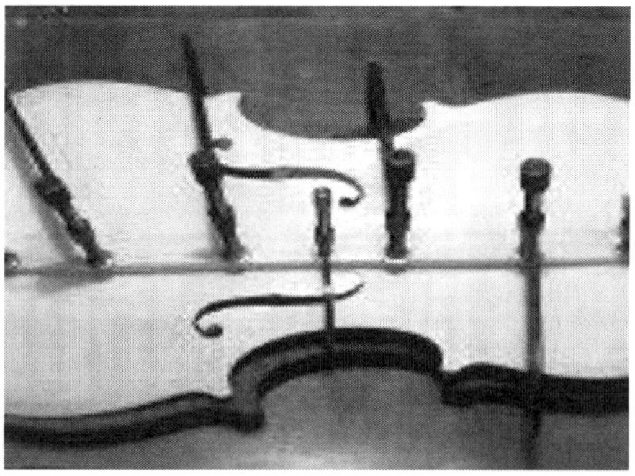

When the glue is dry, the clamps are removed, and the luthier does another plate tuning as described in step 10 above.

Step 13 – The Neck and Scroll — The neck and scroll are carved from one piece of hard wood (usually maple). The luthier draws an outline of the scroll on a wood block. He or she uses a hand or electric saw to cut out the shape.

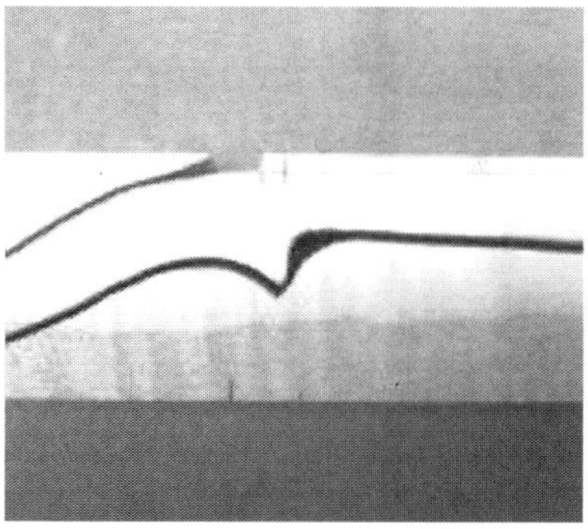

The location for the peg holes is then marked on the cutout.

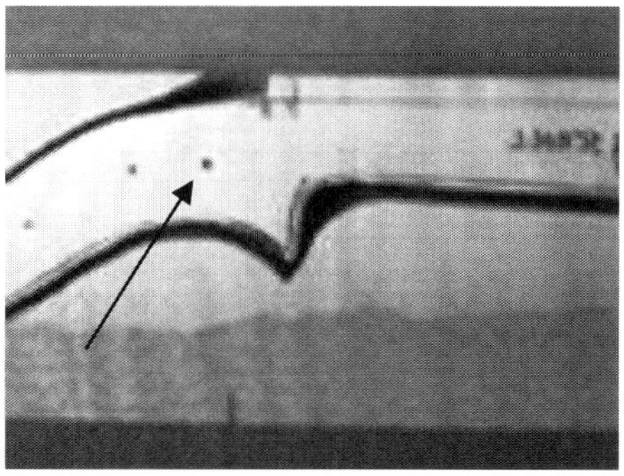

When those steps are completed, sharp knives and files are used to shape the peg box and neck.

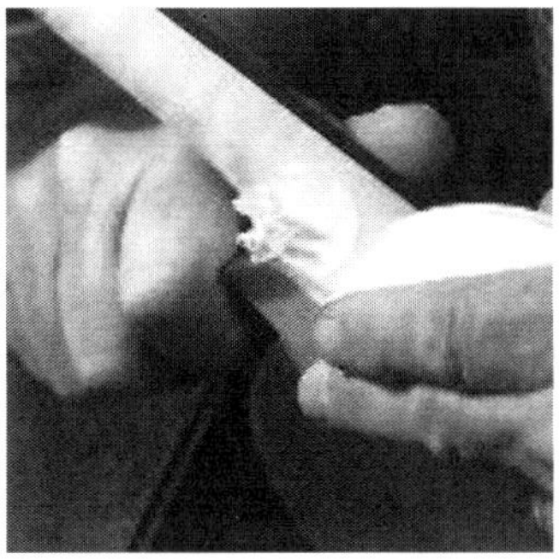  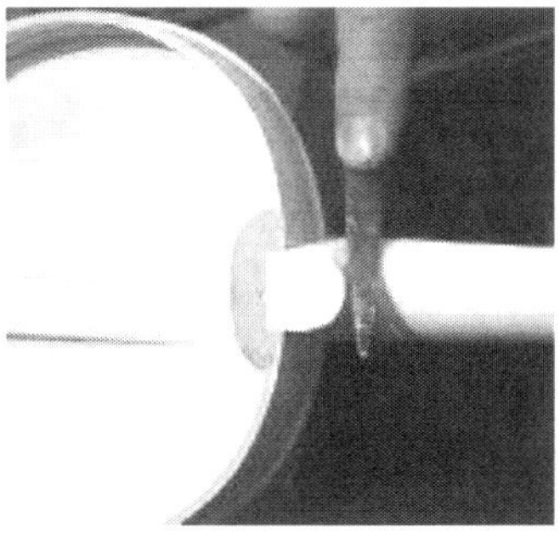

Step 14 – Peg Holes — Peg holes are drilled into the peg box and the pegs are fitted.

Step 15 – The Scroll — It is now time to carve the scroll. This is done using several different saws, scrapers, and carving knives.

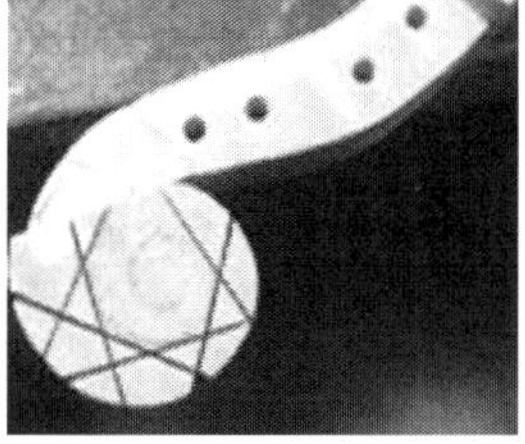  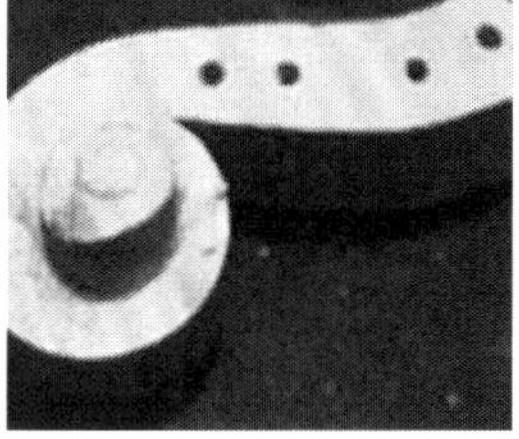

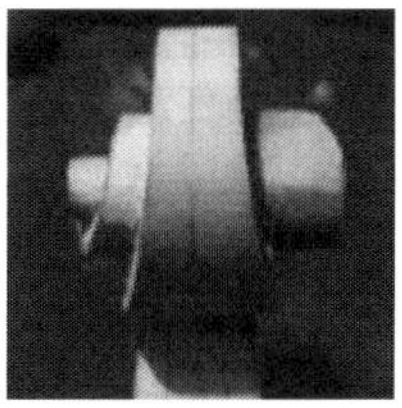  

Step 16 – Carving the Peg Box — The peg box is the space for the pegs with wound strings. The peg box sides (called cheeks) are marked on the block of wood and then the luthier uses a drill to start to remove the wood.

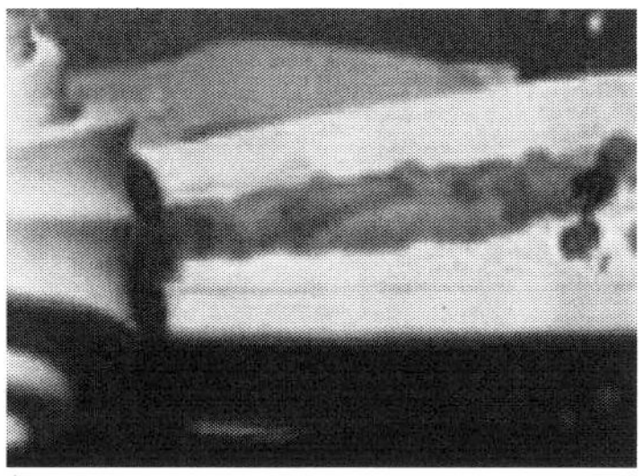

When the extra wood is removed, the luthier switches to a series of sharp carving tools such as chisels and gouges to carve out the remaining wood to form the final peg box shape and size. This is part of the neck which is now ready to be attached to the body of the instrument.

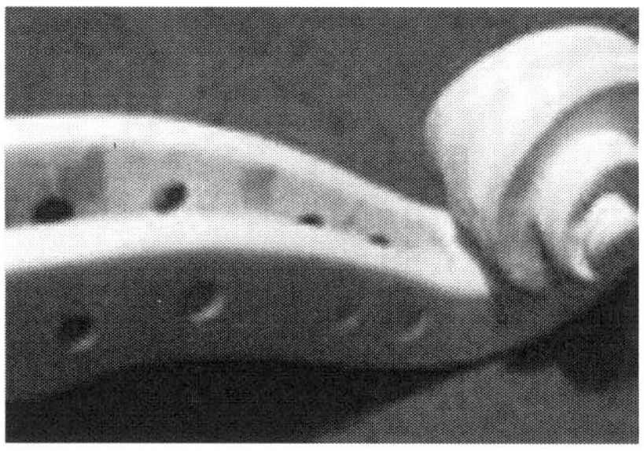

Step 17 – Fitting the Neck to the Body — The neck must be perfectly in line with the violin so that the strings will travel from the peg box over the fingerboard and the bridge to end at the tailpiece. A mortis (opening) is cut into the top block to fit the base of the neck which is then glued in place.

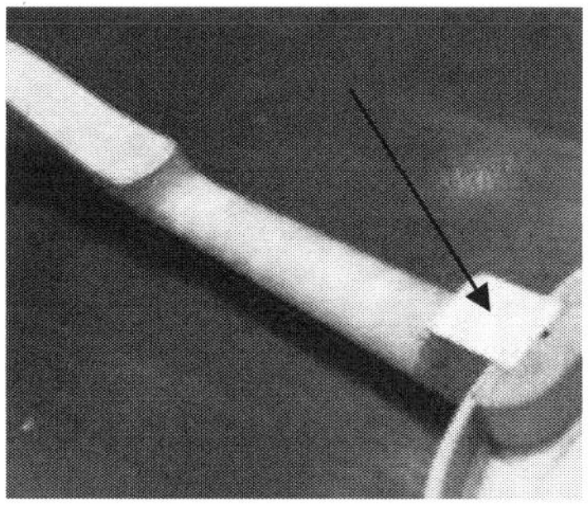

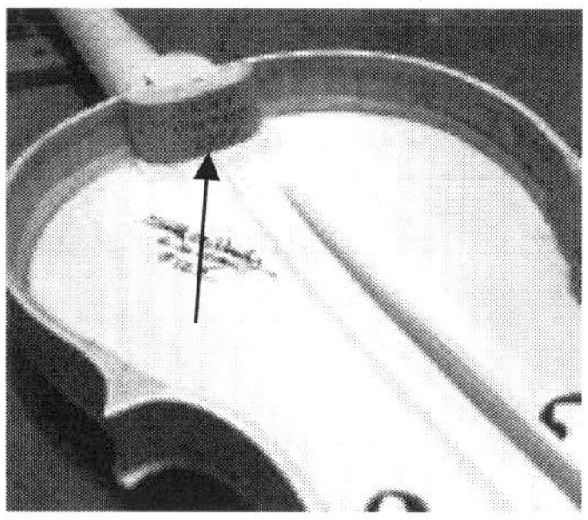

With the neck in place and the glue dry, the back plate is glued on to the ribs.

Step 18 - **The Setup** — To complete the instrument before varnishing, a fingerboard is glued in place.

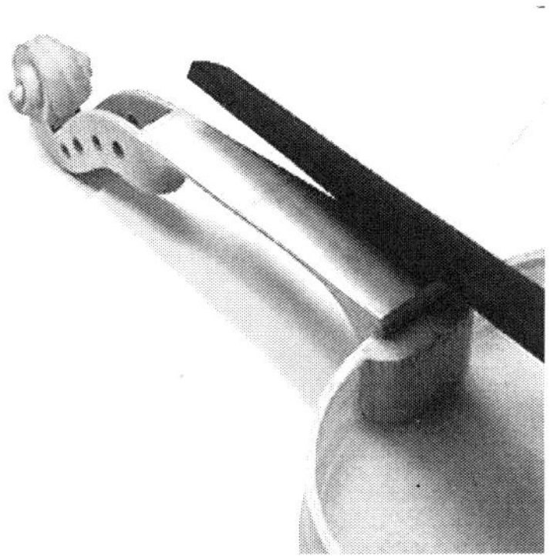

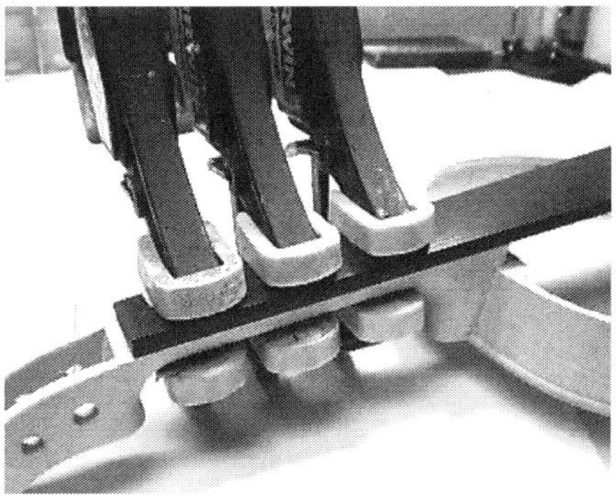

The nut, and saddle are cut, finished and glued in place.

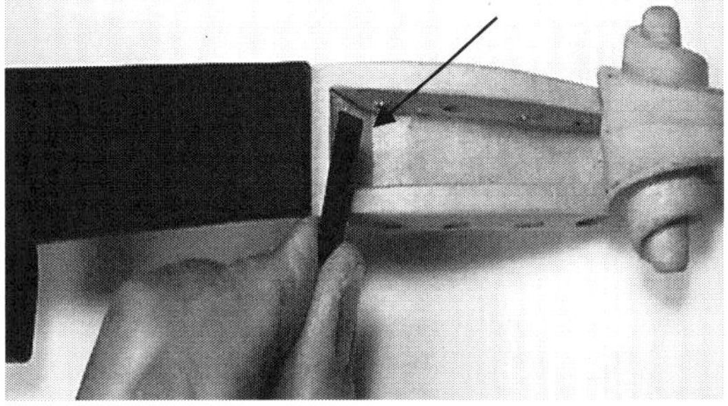

Nut **Saddle**

The peg holes are shaped and made larger (reamed).

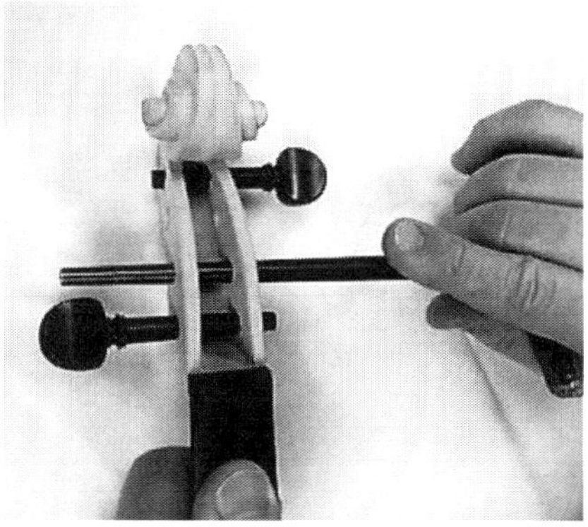

The pegs are shaved to fit the peg holes.

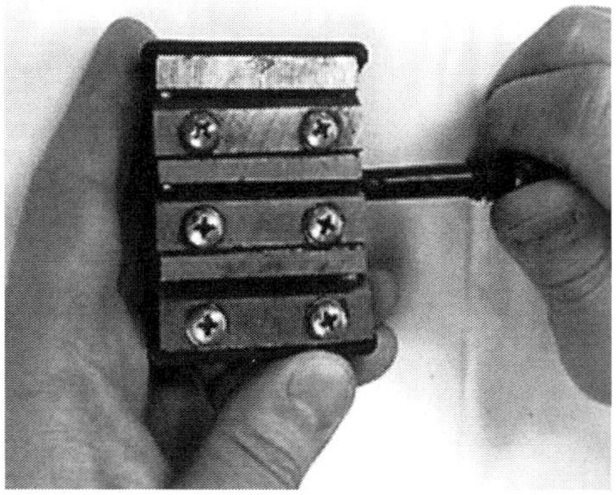

The pegs are installed in the peg box.

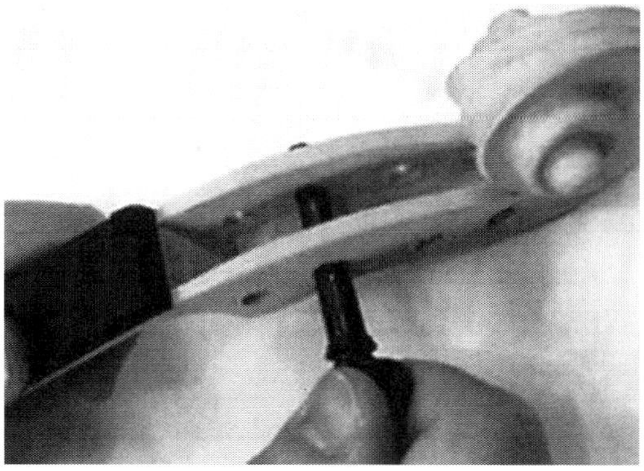

A bridge is cut to shape.

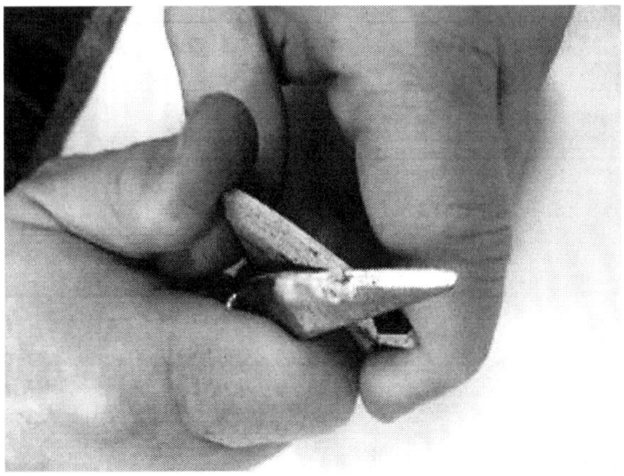

The sound post is cut and put in place.

An end button is fitted and put in the bottom of the violin.

A tailpiece is hooked onto the end button.

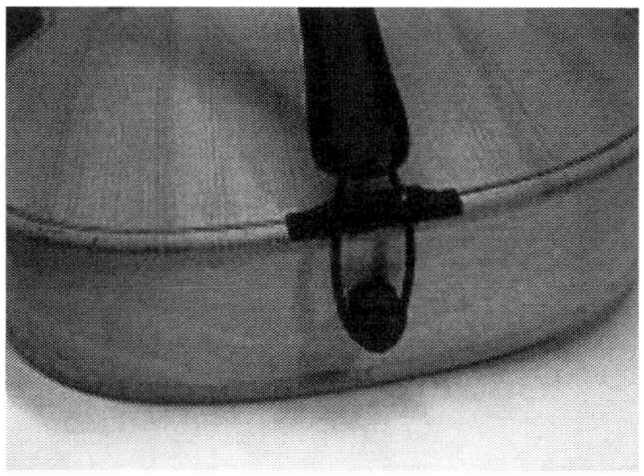

A chin rest in clamped on to the violin's body,

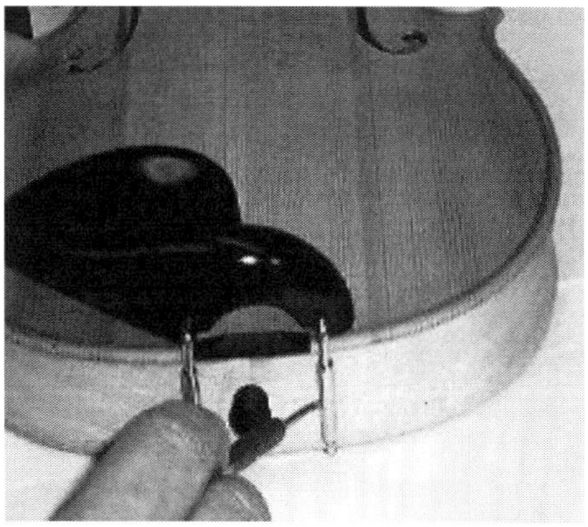

and the violin without a varnish finish, is ready to be strung and tried for sound.

The violin has now been setup "in the white" (without a finish) for the first trial playing. At this time the luthier will make any adjustments needed to improve the sound produced by this new violin.

Step 19 - The Finish — The coating put on the raw wood of the violin after it is complete is called the "finish". The five steps used to finish a violin are:
1. the preparation of the wood,
2. putting on the first (ground) coat of wood treatment on the raw wood,
3. coloring the wood,
4. putting on a protective coating, and finally,
5. polishing the violin.

1. Preparation — To prepare the raw wood, the luthier starts by wetting the surface of the wood to swell the wood grain. The wood is then sanded and scraped until the luthier is satisfied with the appearance of the raw (unfinished) wood.

2. Ground Coat — A ground coat is a liquid sealer that will prepare raw wood to receive color and a finishing product. The ground will fill the pores and cover any spots in the wood. The result will be a smooth surface on which to apply the next step in the finishing process.

3. Color —The luthier chooses and applies color to the violin. He or she may wipe the color on with a cloth, spray it on, or brush it on.

4. Finishing Coat — The finishing coat will most often be varnish. Most luthiers agree that several coats with a fine sanding between each usually has the best result.

5. Polishing — When the varnish is dry, the luthier might improve the finish with hand polishing using any combination of oils, bees' wax, pumice, rotten stone, and turpentine.

Summary — And so, another handmade violin is born. With proper care it can live for centuries. In the hands of professionals, it will provide the world with millions of notes which, when properly combined, will become music. Think back to that first person who plucked the string that made the sound that began the process that led to the violin. What a wonder! Thank you, luthiers of the world, both past and present for your contributions to our musical joy.

NOTES

Chapter 6

What Is the History of the Violin?

Introduction

The first violins began to appear in Italy in about the year 1525. Since the bow was not yet invented, string instruments were played by plucking or strumming the strings. Let's look at some of these "before-the-violin" instruments and see how they developed into the violin we now know.

Lesson One

Plucked Instruments

The Kantele — The kantele is probably one of the earliest of the plucked instruments. It dates back several thousand years to the European countries that border the Baltic sea. The kantele was used to accompany singing and was not a solo instrument like your violin.

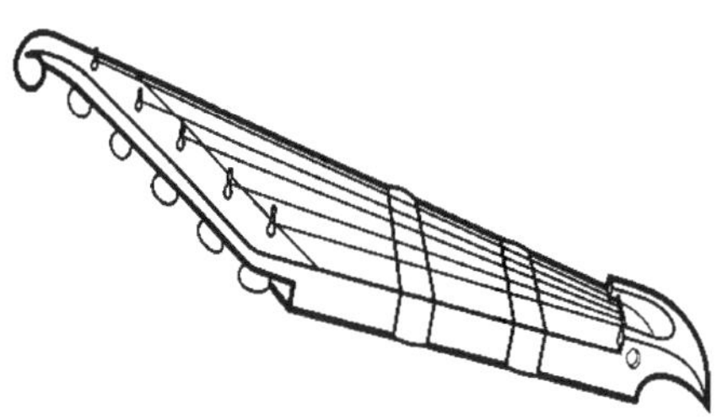

The strings on the kantele were stretched across the instrument's body starting at the tuning pins and ending at a cross bar. Because there was no bridge or nut, the sound was more like a bell than a violin.

The strings were tuned to either a major or minor scale. The kantele was placed on a flat surface or on the player's lap where it could be strummed or plucked with the fingers or a guitar-like pick called a plectrum.

The "U" Shaped Lyre — The picture on the right is a "U" shaped lyre. Notice the shape of the instrument starting from the two arms at the top that form a "U". Look at the body and you will see the

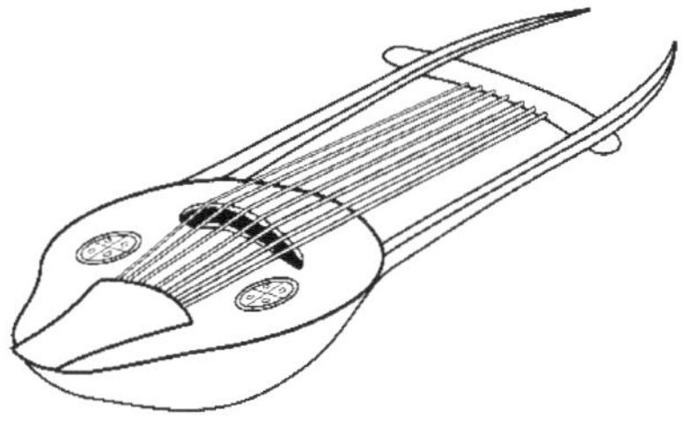

strings traveling over a bridge, a sound hole on either side of the bridge like the violin ***"f"*** holes, and the strings attached to a tail piece.

There is no fingerboard. The different pitches came from the thickness and tightness of the string. Look at your violin and you will see the same idea. Your E string is the thinnest and, as such, the highest pitched. Your A string is next in thickness and is lower pitched than the E string. The D and G strings follow that pattern.

As you can see by the shape of the instrument, it would not be possible to bow the strings. The strings had to be plucked.

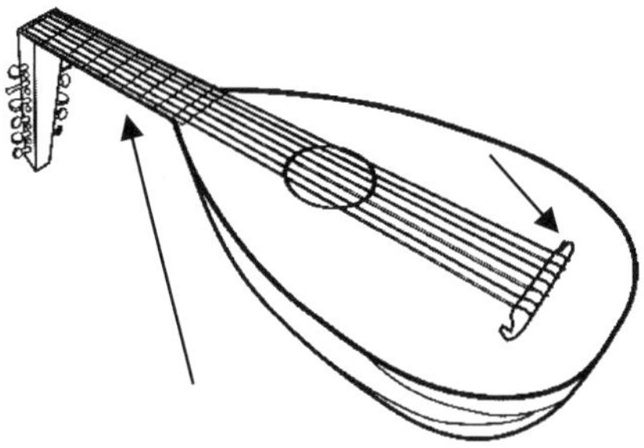

The Lute — The lute begins to look something like a violin. At the top it has a peg box and tuning pegs attached to strings which travel over the nut. A big difference between the lute and the violin is in the frets (metal strips) on the fingerboard similar to those found on a guitar. Also note that the strings are connected directly to the bridge instead of passing over a bridge as do those on your violin.

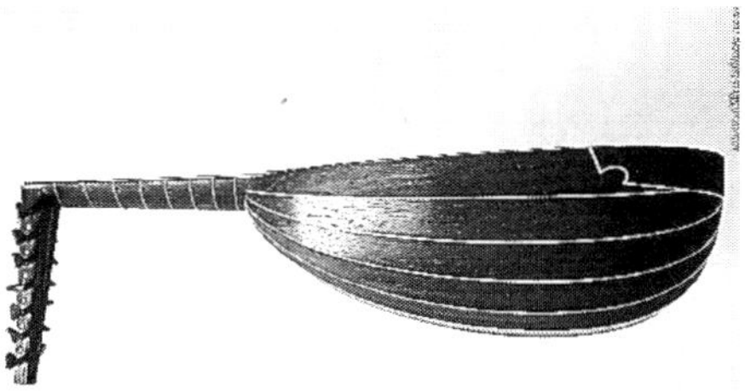

Another difference between the lute and your violin is the shape of the body and the fact that the back of the lute body was made of strips of wood instead of one or two pieces of wood on the back of a violin.

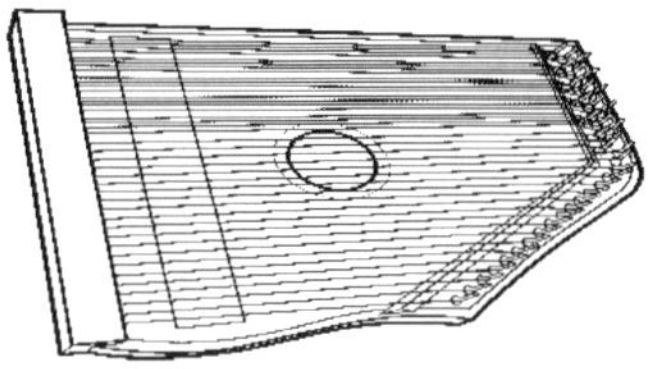

The Zither — Zither is a name given to string instruments that have strings stretched across a sound board. The zither is played on a flat surface or on the player's lap.

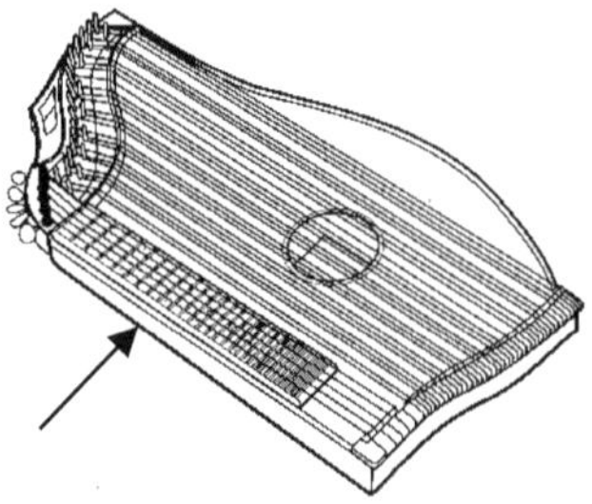

This instrument was very popular because it was easy to make and play. Because of this popularity, a number of different designs were developed. On the top right you see an early zither with no fingerboard. The bottom right shows a zither with a fretted fingerboard under only five strings.

Timeline — The following timeline shows some of the early plucked instruments as they might have appeared through history.

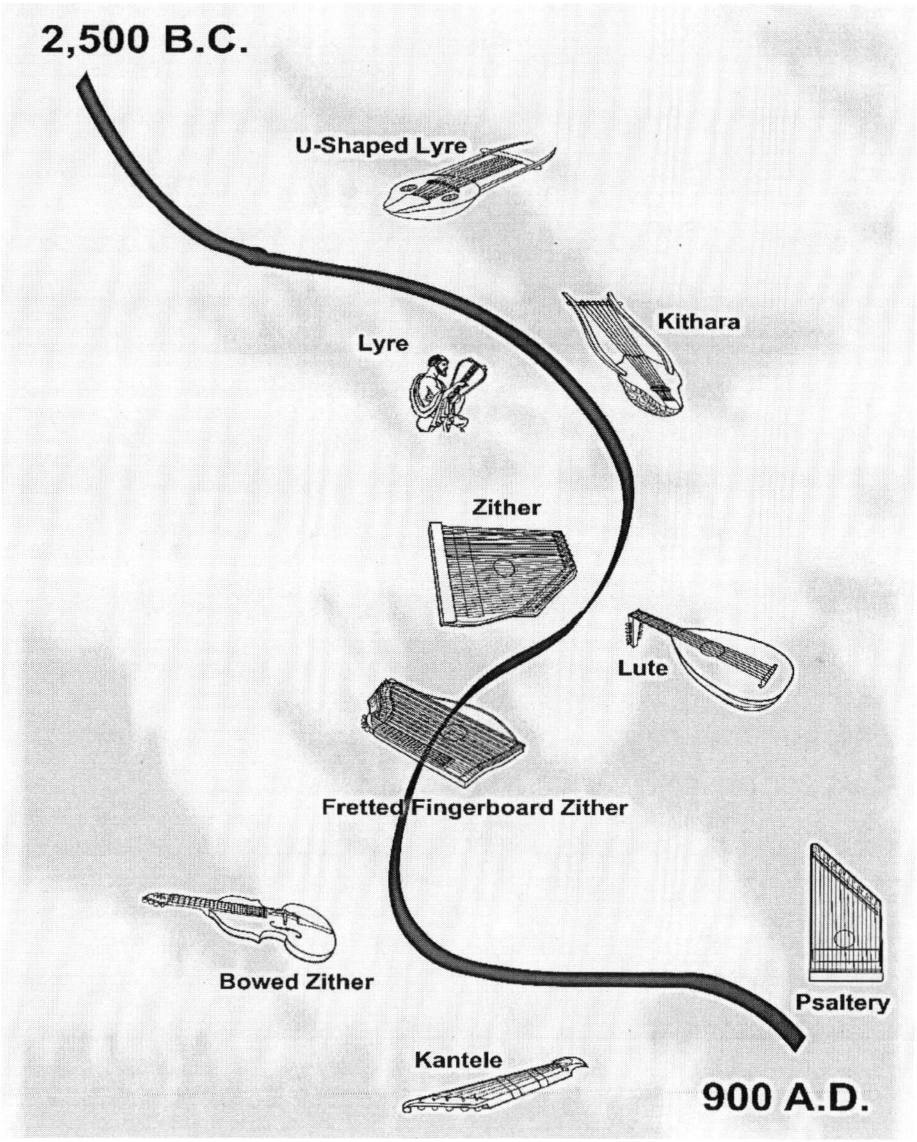

Lesson Two

Early Bowed Instruments

The Bowed Zither — The bowed zither arrives. Does it look familiar? Yes, we finally begin to see our violin appear. The zither has a slightly different shape but a body shape that will allow a bow to pass over the strings, ***"f"*** holes on either side of the bridge, four pegs slightly different from those on your violin, and a finger board but with frets like a guitar.

At some point in history, musicians began understanding that by rubbing a tacky stick or chord across a string, they were producing a richer sound than that produced by plucking the string. And so, began the early but not yet violin-like bowed instruments.

In about 900 A.D. instruments with a body, fingerboard, a peg box, and tunable strings, began to appear. Let's look at some of these instruments to see if we can find more signs of a violin's developing.

The Rebab — The rebab was an African bowed string instrument. The rebab was usually constructed with a pear-shaped body that was hollowed out from a block of wood. A thin sheet of wood or animal hide was then attached to the hollowed-out section to act as a top. Unlike the modern violin, the fingerboard was part of the body instead of a separate piece attached to the instrument.

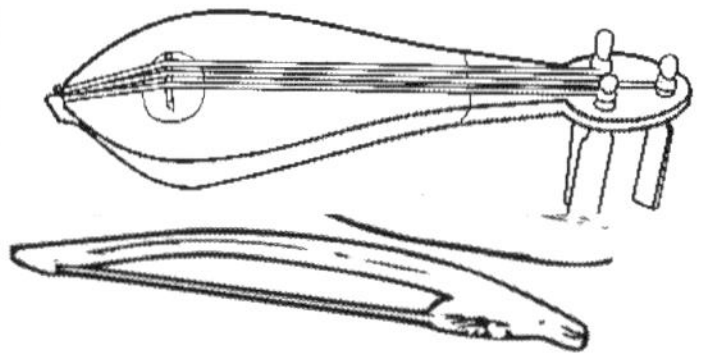

Rebabs usually had two or three strings that were played with a bow. As far back as the 8th century, the rebab was being played in North Africa, the Middle East and in Europe.

The Spike Fiddle — Another form of rebab, a spike fiddle, had a round body. The neck was a round pole that supported the strings and extended down through the body to form an endpin. The player held the spike fiddle upright, resting it on the ground or on his or her lap.

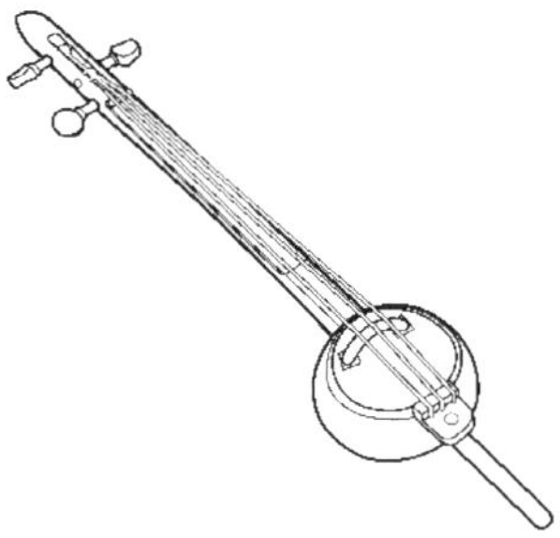

The Rebec — The rebec existed in Europe during the 15th and 16th centuries. The rebec is like a rebab except for the body. The body of the rebec was made from the dried shell of a plant. This shell is called a gourd.

We now begin to see the beginnings of a violin in the rebec. Up to now, most string instrument fingerboards were part of the instrument's body. Like the violin to follow, the rebec's fingerboard was made separately and then attached to the body of the instrument.

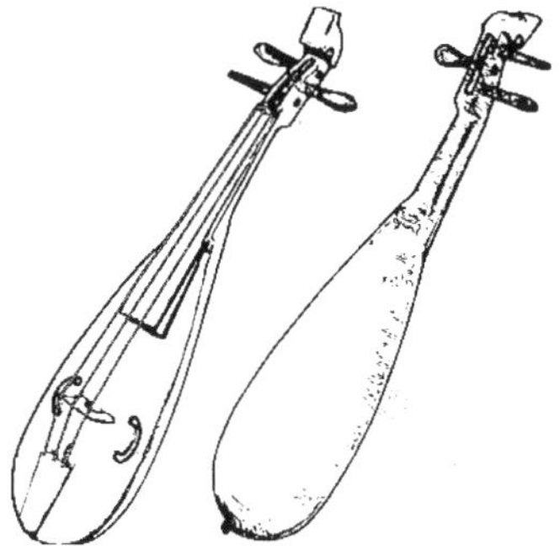

The Vielle — The vielle appeared in France during the Medieval period from the thirteenth to the fifteenth century. This instrument was closer in design to the modern violin. Rather than having a gourd-shaped body, as did the rebec, the vielle's body was constructed like your violin with a wider upper and lower section (bout) and a narrower mid-section. This mid-section allowed a player to use a bow more easily.

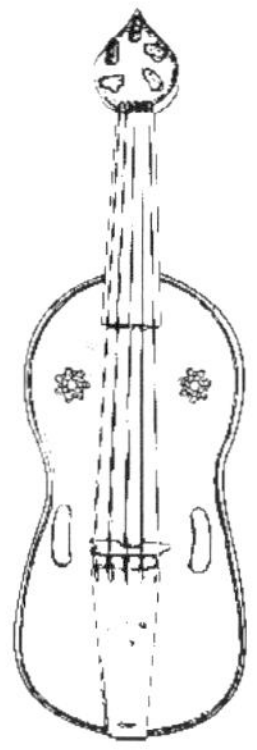

The body of the vielle was longer and wider than that of your violin and had a flat peg box. The pegs were set on the top of the peg box facing upward. The vielle had five strings.

The timeline below shows the second phase in the evolution of string instruments.

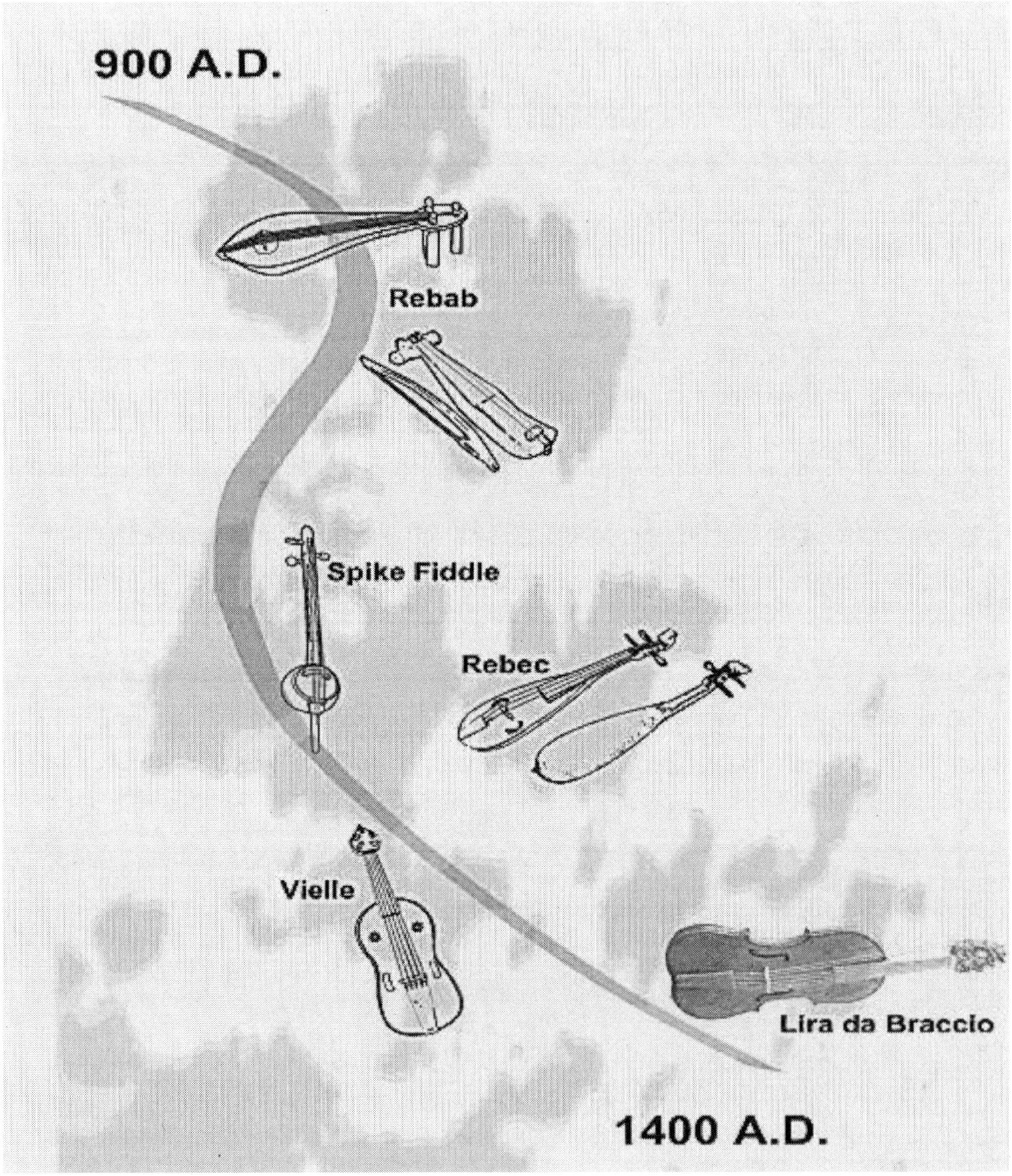

Lesson Three

The Birth of the Violin

The Lira da Braccio (Lyre for the Arm) — Following the vielle was the lira da braccio (Italian for lyre of the arm) which first appeared in Italy. This was a bowed string instrument more closely resembling your violin but with a wider fingerboard.

The lira da braccio could have as many as seven strings. Four were tuned to E, A, D, and G over a fingerboard as are those of your violin. Another low D string was also placed over the fingerboard, and two other strings ran along the side of the fingerboard.

The tuning pegs on the lira da braccio were installed on the top of a leaf-shaped peg box instead of on the sides as on your violin. The picture above is of a lira da braccio in the Kunsthistorisches Museum, Musikinstrumente, Vienna, Austria.

This instrument was difficult to play because of the number of strings which were used to play melody and chords at the same time. This led musicians to begin to look at a newer instrument called the violin.

The First Violin? — We do not know exactly who made the first violin. Gasparo da Salo of Brescia, Italy (C.1540-1609) and Andrea Amati of Cremona, Italy (C.1525-1611) were violin makers (luthiers) who were making violins at about the same time. We really do not know who was first so let's give them both credit for being among the first luthiers to make violins. At this time in history, violin makers began to appear in many different parts of Europe.

Lesson Four

The Schools

When you hear the word school, you will probably think of the building that you go to for your violin lesson or to study other subjects. The word school can also have another meaning. A school can be a place where people who are interested in a particular subject, in this case violin making, gather and live in a particular area to practice their art. The goal is to develop their skills and broaden knowledge in their subject.

The violin makers from the mid-fifteen hundreds to about 1725 gathered in "schools" where they developed and refined the violin to become the instrument we know and enjoy today.

Over a period of some 200 years, a number of such schools began to appear throughout Europe. Among them were the Brescian, Cremonese, Neapolitan, Tyrolean, and French schools. Each is named for the geographic location where it was centered. The following map shows the location of some of these "schools" in Europe.

(C.1784-1875)
Lupot, Vuillaume

(C.1620-1743)
Klotz, Stainer

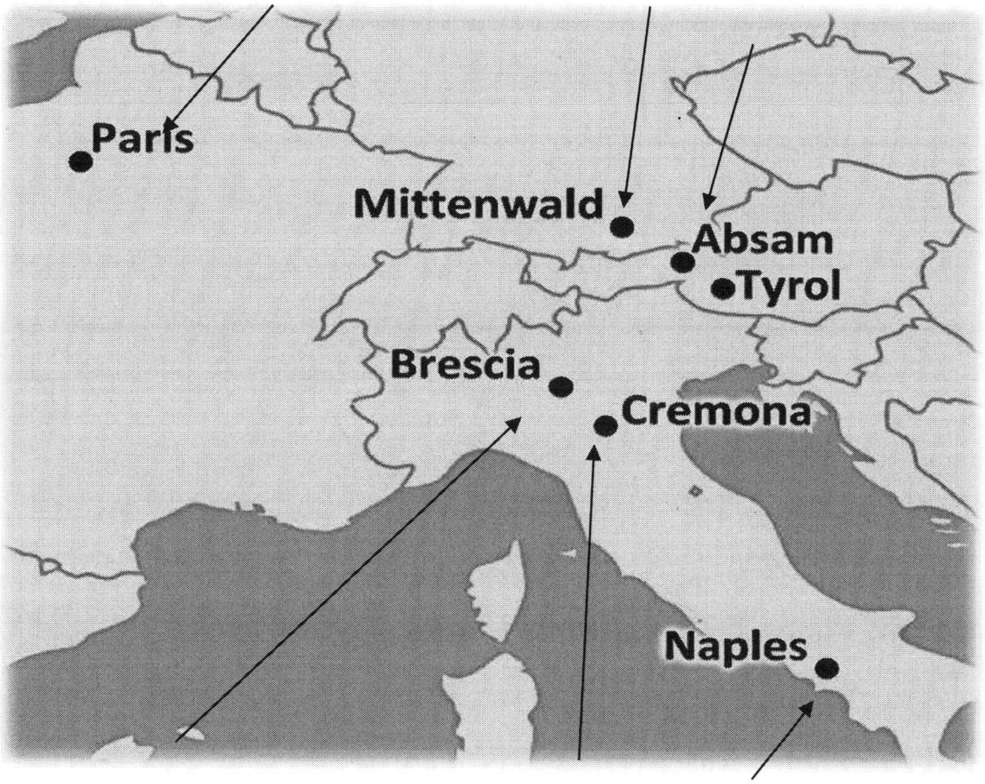

Gasparo da Salo
Maggini, Rogeri
(C.1585-1895)

Amati, Bergonzi, Gagliano,**
Guarneri, Ruggieri, Stradivari
(C. 1541-1744)

***Bergonzi & Gagliano worked in Cremona and Naples**

Let's now look into where the violin makers worked and what they did.

Cremonese School — Cremona, Italy

Andrea Amati (1525-1611) was the principal figure in the Cremonese school of violin making. His early works consisted of rebecs and other string instruments that preceded the violin. At this point in time, historians began to see evidence showing the development of other instruments of the string family. Andrea's family consisted of Antonio, Girolamo, Nicolo, and Girolamo II, all of whom carried on the Amati tradition of making extraordinary string instruments up to 1740. Many of the instruments they made are still being played today.

Antonio Stradivari (1644-1737) was, and still is, the most famous violin maker in history. During his lifetime, Stradivari made more than one thousand instruments.

Francesco Ruggieri (1620-1695) is recognized for improving the design of the cello.

Carlo Bergonzi (1683-1747) was a neighbor and then student of Stradivari. Bergonzi became Stradivari's repair technician.

Brescian School — Brescia, Italy

Brescia is the second largest city in the Lombardy region of northern Italy, at the base of the Alps. In the period between 1585 and 1895, Brescia became a center for master luthiers. In Brescia, the viola da braccia (of the arm), viola da gamba (of the leg), and many other viols that had evolved up to that time became the models for the violin, viola, cello, and double bass. The luthiers of the Brescian school were considered to be among the best instrument makers. Unfortunately, an outbreak of a deadly disease spread throughout the region, killing most of the population.

Gasparo da Salo (1542-1609) — Gasparo developed a longer shaped violin which produced a more forceful sound. He also made a number of other string instruments in the viola, cello, and double bass categories.

Giovanni Paolo Maggini (1580-1630) —Maggini became a student of Gasparo da Salo. At about twenty years of age, Maggini began to develop his own violin designs with larger sound holes and a lower curving top. Maggini made about seventy-five instruments, mostly violins and violas, two cellos, and what might possibly be one of the first double basses.

Neapolitan School — Naples, Italy

In the south of Italy, the area of Naples was growing. This growth increased the demand for musical instruments and resulted in the development of the Neapolitan School of violin making.

Alessandro Gagliano (1640-1725) — Alessandro Gagliano and his family made instruments for almost three hundred years up to the year 1925. Alessandro was the head of the family and is known for developing a brilliantly clear varnish with a beautiful red tint.

Tyrolean School — Mittenwald, Germany

During that same period the Tyrolean School grew where Jacob Stainer (1620-1683) and Matthias Klotz (1656-1743) were the most important luthiers.

Jacob Stainer (1620-1683) was one of the most important luthiers of his time. He developed a design for his instruments which featured a higher arch on the top and back. He was also noted for his unique scrolls which often featured carved heads in place of the traditional scroll shape.

Matthias Klotz (1656-1743) used his business skills to develop a complete violin industry. Like the Gagliano family, Klotz's business also became the family business, producing many instruments which are still available today.

French School — Mirecourt, France

In 1635 there were 43 luthiers in Mirecourt, France. About a century and a half later, Nicholas Lupot (1784-1824) and Jean-Baptiste Vuillaume (1798-1875) were best known for their ability to produce excellent violins based on the designs of previous masters. By the 20th century, Mirecourt had become the center of the violin making business.

Nicholas Lupot (1784-1824) was most noted for copying the Stradivari design as well as designs of other masters. Nicholas did not distinguish himself so much for his originality but rather for the delicate refinement he added to the patterns of others.

Jean-Baptiste Vuillaume (1798-1875) was able to copy the styles and varnishes of the master luthiers of the past. In 1828 he started his own business where he sold his reproductions along with other high-quality instruments.

Summary — The "schools" of violin making mentioned above are only some of many that came into being throughout Europe beginning in the sixteenth century. Venice and Absam (Austria) schools along with other lesser known clusters of luthiers on every level developed the violin, viola, cello, and double bass that we enjoy today.

Chapter 7

How Are Violin Bows Made?

Introduction — A violin bow looks like a stick with hair attached to it. In fact, it is made up of between thirteen and fifteen parts. The parts we see most easily are the stick, hair, and frog. Not easily seen are the hidden parts that keep the bow together.

As you read this chapter, have your bow handy and look at each bow part as it is discussed.

The Materials — The materials needed to make a bow are:

1. wood for the stick, usually Pernambuco with a straight, dense grain;
2. ebony for the frog;
3. metal for the fittings;
4. a sheet of mother of pearl for the slide;
5. a few hard-wood plugs and wedges, and;
6. a hank of horsehair.

The Stick — The first step in making a bow is choosing the wood to be used for the stick. The best bows are usually made with Pernambuco, a hard wood grown in Brazil. The bow maker (archetier) starts with a rectangular strip of wood the length of the bow. This is called a straight blank. He or she then checks for defects in the grain such as a knot or worm hole.

https://fiddlershop.com/blog/Pernambuco-Violin-Bow-info

The blank is then roughly formed into an eight-sided (octagonal) shape.

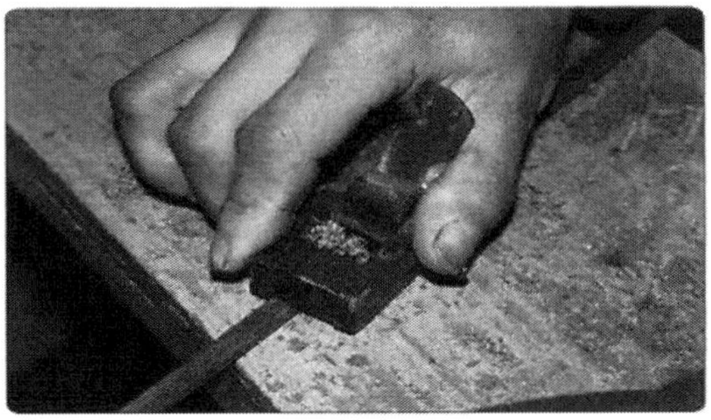

The Head or Tip — After the stick is formed, the bow maker carves the tip of the bow.

When the tip is completed, a bone or ivory tip is glued in place and a hole (mortise) is cut into its base to hold the tip end of the hair.

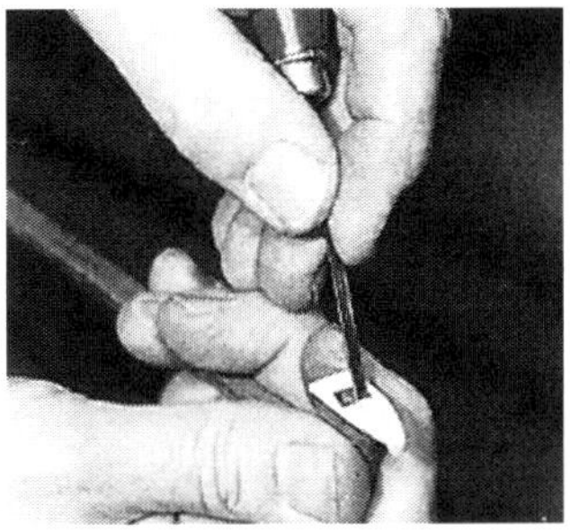

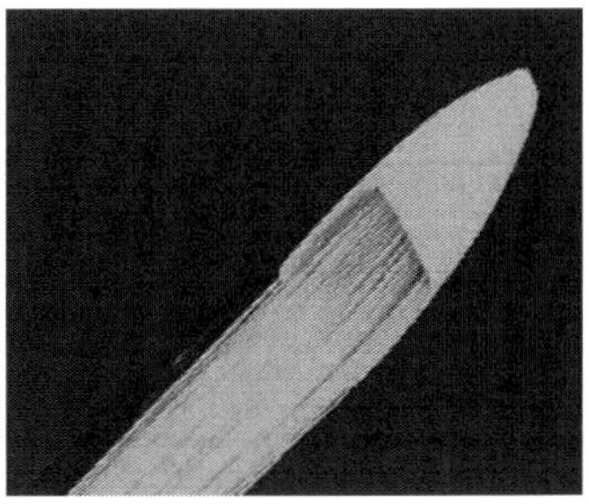

A mortise (hole) is cut into the other end of the stick to fit the frog.

The Frog — The bow maker begins shaping a blank piece of ebony wood into a shape which is wider on the bottom than at the top. The sides of the wood are shaped to curve in slightly.

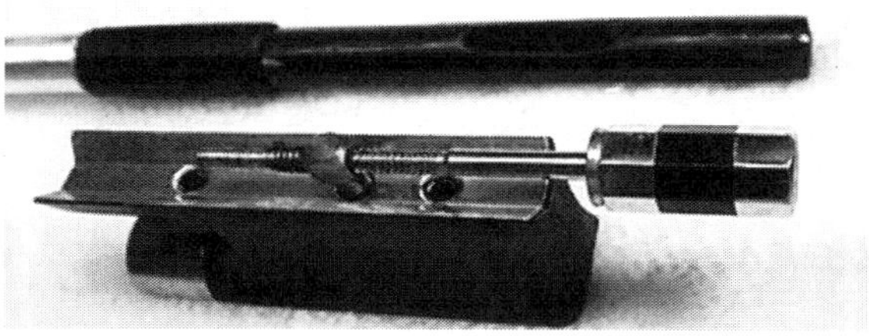

He or she cuts a mortise into the frog in which the bow hair will be placed. Below is a frog with a mortise which is cut out and ready to accept hair.

The front of the frog will then be shaped into a "U" which faces the tip of the bow.

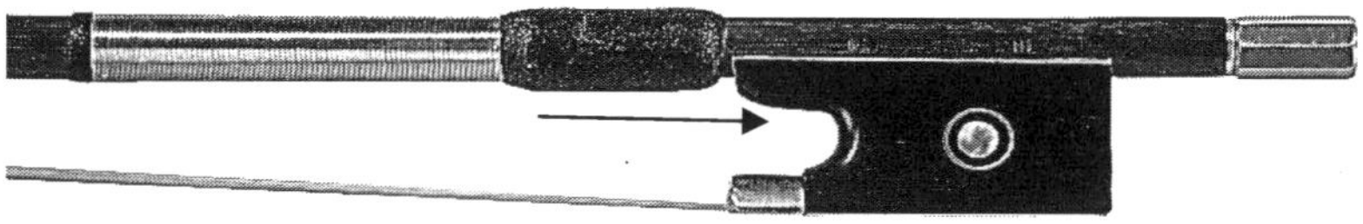

Below is a finished frog with the hair installed. The arrow points to a metal half-round band called a ferrule which is placed at the end of the frog.

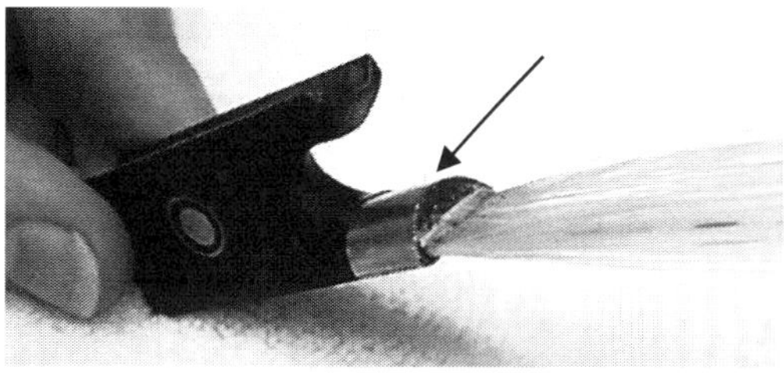

On the underside of the frog behind the ferrule is a mother of pearl slide (A) which covers the mortise and holds the bow hair in place. Continuing from that slide is a silver plate (B) which travels up the back of the frog to its top. On either side of the frog, a mother of pearl eye (C) is placed as a decoration.

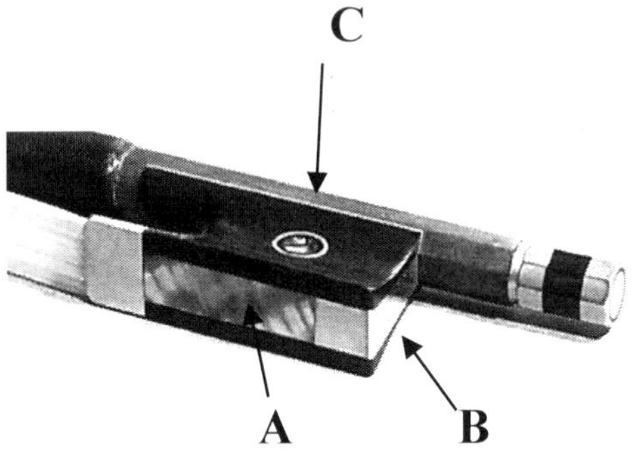

Fitting the Frog — The top of the frog is shaped to fit the stick. To strengthen the frog and ease its sliding back and forth on the stick, a strip of metal called an underslide is placed on the top of the frog to help support it and prevent cracking.

When finished, the frog is made up of a screw (A) and eyelet (B) with a button (C) on the end of the screw. The eyelet is screwed into the top of the frog. The screw (A) goes into the eyelet (B) and the button (C) is used to turn the screw.

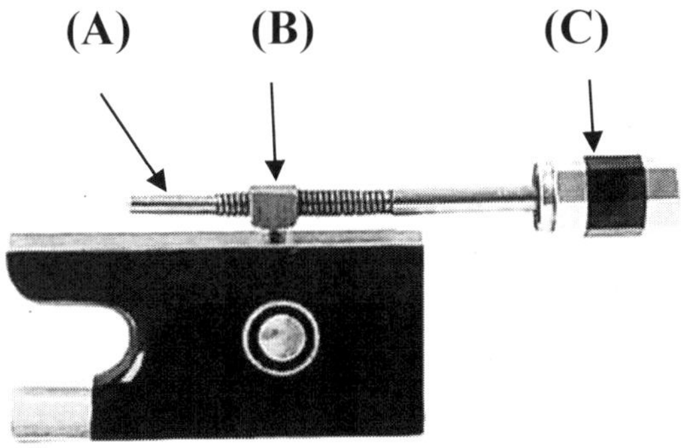

Creating the Curve (Camber) in a Bow Stick — To put the curve in a violin bow stick, the bow maker (archetier) heats the stick using a soft flame such as that from an alcohol lamp. When the stick has reached the proper temperature, it will begin to bend more easily. At that point it is pressed against a form until the takes on the curve needed. The stick is then cooled and will keep the curved shape.

The Bow Grip — Just forward of the frog on the stick is a wrapping or bow grip which can be made of almost any material that can be wrapped around a stick. Most commonly used are whalebone, silver, leather, or rubber.

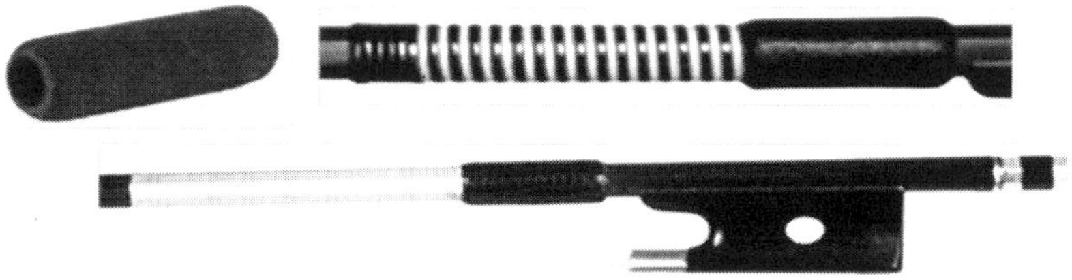

Completing the Stick — Let's review the work that has been done up to this point:

1. The archetier started with a "blank" strip of wood for the stick.

2. The stick was carved and shaped.

3. A frog was cut from a block of ebony wood.

4. A mortise was cut into the block to receive the bow hair.

5. The metal parts were added to the frog.

6. The tip of the stick was carved and shaped.

7. An ivory tip was glued on to the tip.

8. A mortise was cut into the tip to receive the bow hair.

9. The stick was heated and curved to create a proper camber.

10. A grip was added to the stick just forward of the frog.

Hairing the Bow — The next step is hairing the bow. Use the diagram below along with your own bow as a guide while you read about the process.

To hair a bow, a hank of horse hair (A) is combed so that all hairs are parallel to one another. One end of the hank is then tied and forced securely into a box-shaped cutout (mortise) at the tip of the bow (B). The hair is held in place by a wooden, wedge-shaped plug (C) that is cut to exactly fit the space and hold the hair in place.

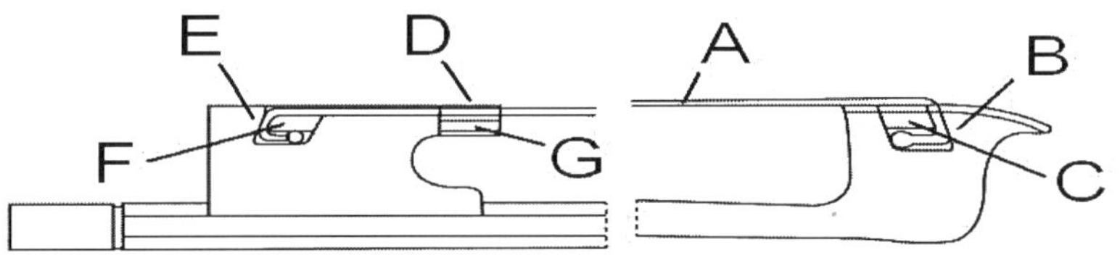

A ferrule, (metal band) (D) is placed over the hair which is stretched along the bow, tied at the other end, and set into a box-shaped cutout in the frog (E). A wooden wedge-shaped plug is placed into the box (F) to keep the hair in place. A slide and another wooden wedge are placed between the ferrule and the frog (G) to help distribute the hairs equally and to keep them in place.

Now the archetier will make the final adjustments to the stick to be sure it is straight, balanced, flexible, has the proper camber, and that the frog works properly. He or she will then color and polish the stick.

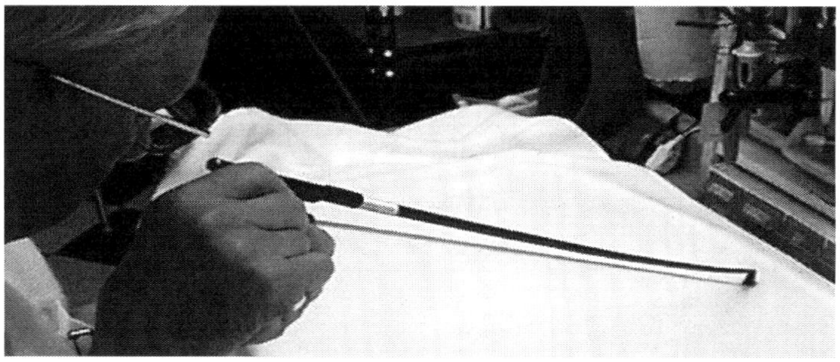

Summary — A bow is an important part of your producing sound on a violin. For this reason, the quality of the hair and wood used, how the wood is formed into a well-balanced stick with proper camber (curve), and correct weight and balance are most important.

NOTES

Chapter 8

What Is the History of Violin Bows?

The discovery that rubbing something against a string can make a sound probably resulted in the very earliest bow being made. Drawings dating as far back as the eighth century show cords and hair tied or connected to bow-shaped sticks. That shape would allow the cords or hairs to have free contact with a string on an instrument and, when rubbed against the string, produce a vibration (sound).

The master archetier (bow maker) Eitan Hoffer operates a shop in Israel where he makes bows for ancient instruments. Below are some pictures of Mr. Hoffer's bows which illustrate the shapes that came before the bows we now use.

The following examples of ancient bows were reproduced with permission of Eitan Hoffer, Bow Maker (www.hoffer-bows. com).

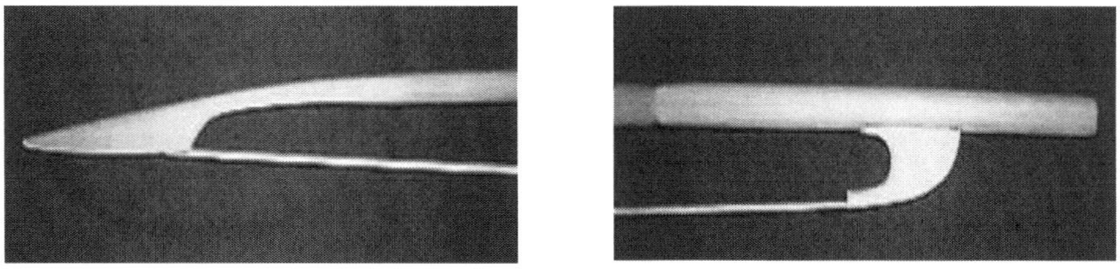

Renaissance Viol Bow Made from yew wood.

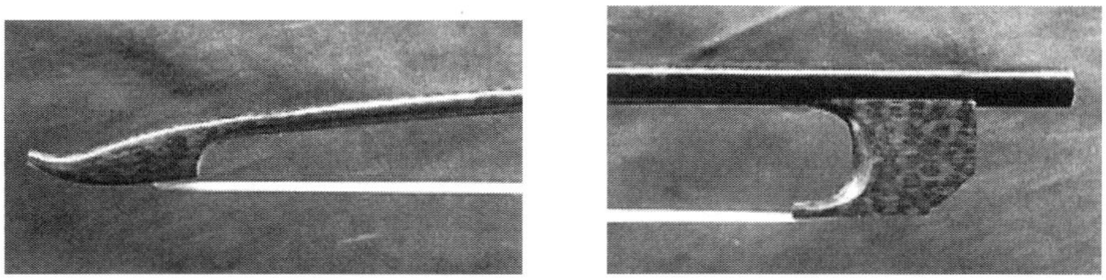

Short Violin Bow
Copy of an original Italian bow produced at the end of the 16th century.

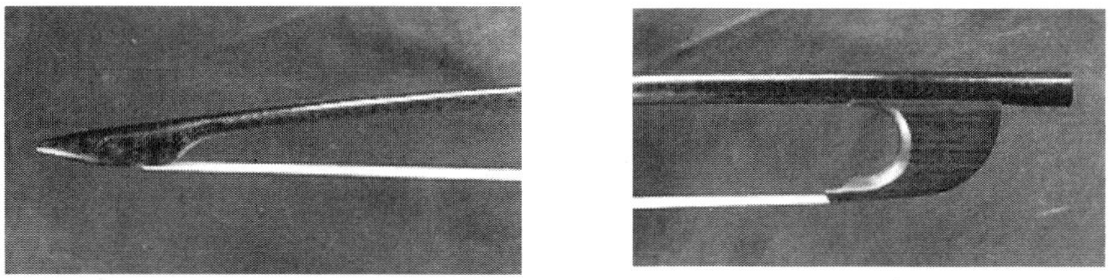

17th Century Style Violin Bow
Made from snakewood, this bow is almost 26 inches long.

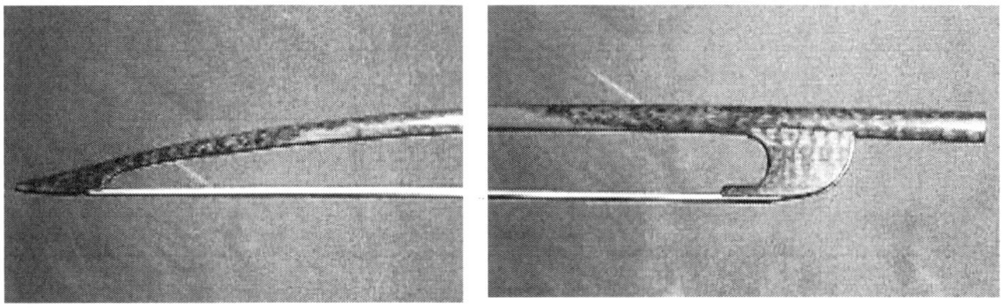

17th Century Short Bow

A reproduction of a bow from the year 1680. Look at the difference in size of the frog as compared to the bow above.

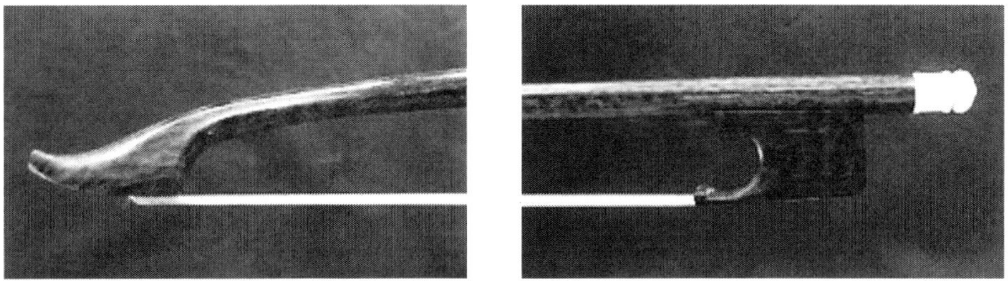

French 18th Century Violin Bow with Screw Mechanism

Made from snakewood, this is one of the early examples of a movable frog.

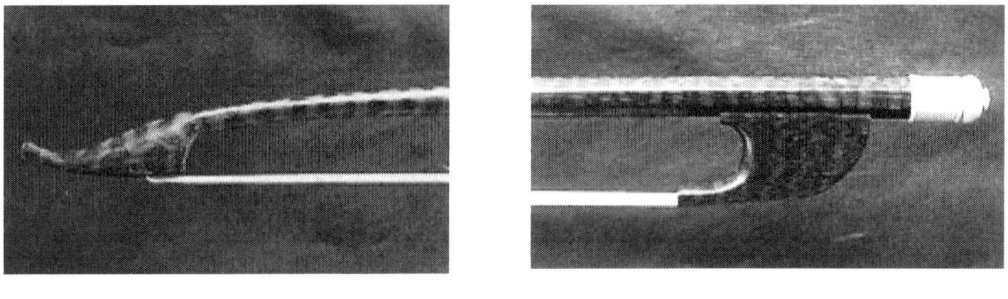

Violin "Long Sonata Bow" (c. 1720)

A copy of the original bow used for playing early 18th century music like that of J. S. Bach.

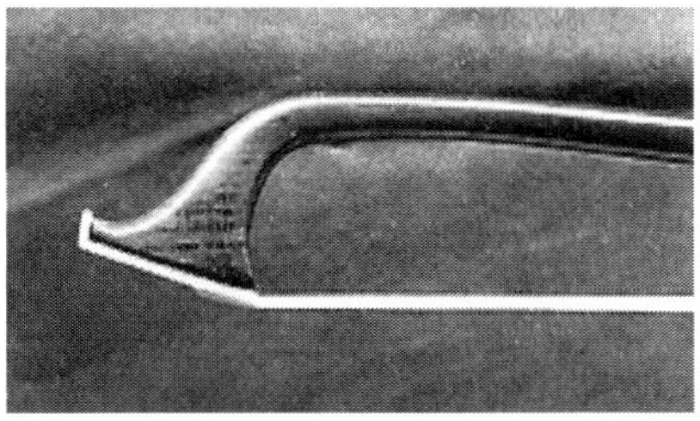 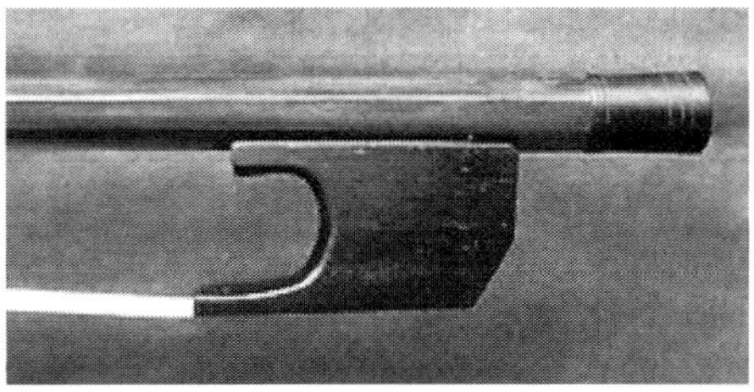

Classical Bow
Based on an original bow by N. Duchaine (c. 1765).

The Bow You Now Use

The bow you use to play your violin is a very important part of the sound-making process. You use your bow to control the tone quality, clarity, volume, phrasing and all the musical sounds you are making. You, your bow, and your violin are partners in the act of making music. Because of the importance of this three-way partnership, you must give credit to those bowmakers from the past who improved the ancient bows we see above to develop the bow you now use.

François Xavier Tourte (1747-1835) had the greatest effect on the development of the bow you use today. Trained to make violins by his father Nicolas Pierre (1700-1765), François also began work on improving the bow. He changed the balances, increased the weight of the frog and tip, and changed the bow's length. Tourte also refined the process for creating the camber (curve) in the bow stick by using heat instead of the carving method used at that time.

Added to that list of improvements, François invented the moveable frog using the screw and eye mechanism which you now use to tighten or loosen your bow hair. He also began the use of a wooden wedge between the hair and the ferrule to spread the hairs at the frog. This small but very important addition keeps the individual hairs firmly in place and parallel to one another rather than clumping together.

An interesting story about François tells about his passion for perfection. François would destroy any bow made in his shop which in his judgment was not perfect. The result was the possible loss of some extraordinary bows which, although not perfect enough in his eyes to enjoy life, would probably serve us as great tools. His bow design became the model for all the prominent bow makers to follow.

The three most famous bowmakers after Tourte were Ludwig Bausch (1805-1871), François Voirin (1833-1885), and Eugene Sartory (1871-1946).

Ludwig Christian August Bausch (1805-1871) followed Tourte as a maker of very fine violin bows. Ludwig lived and worked in Germany where he and his two sons carried on the Tourte fine bow making art until 1874.

François Nicolas Voirin (1833-1885) was a French maker of very fine bows. Many violinists feel that these bows are the best made. Voirin redesigned the Tourte bow by thinning out the tip, changing the camber (curve) of the stick and making it thinner at the heel (frog end).

Eugene Nicolas Sartory (1871-1946) was also a French maker of fine bows. His bows were made with stronger thicker sticks and wider tips than the bows made by Voirin and Bausch.

Summary — At some point in the development of civilization, it was learned that rubbing a rough stick against a tight string would produce a sound. Ancient drawings and paintings which contain pictures of instruments and their bows show bow-shaped sticks with hair or chords connected to the stick on both ends. A musician could rub that chord or hair against a tight string and produce sound. From that point on, people's creative ability took over to develop the bows that you use to play your violin today.

Chapter 9

A Dictionary for Violin Students

During your studies, you will come across unfamiliar words that are related to your violin or bow. This dictionary lists the words in alphabetical order and their meanings.

Terms Used for Bowing Directions

The universal language for music is Italian; however, other languages are also used.

Arco (Italian) — Use the bow to play this section.

Au Talon (French) — Play this passage at the frog end of the bow.

Avec le Bois (French) — Use the bow stick in place of the bow hair to bow the string.

Bow — An arch-shaped stick with horsehair or manufactured hair that is stretched from one end of the stick to the other. The hair is drawn across a violin string to produce sound.

Brazilwood — A type of wood used to make bows.

Col Legno Battuto (Italian) — Strike the string with the wooden bow stick using a bouncing motion.

Collé (French) — Use a light short bow stroke. Attack from above using a brief contact with the string followed by a clean release upward.

Col Legno Tratto (Italian) — Use the bow stick in place of the bow hair to bow the string.

Détaché (French) — Bow detached notes smoothly with no pause between them.

Détaché Lance (French) — Bow detached notes smoothly with a slight pause between them. The notes are not separate.

Flautando (Italian) — Bow close to or slightly over the edge of the fingerboard. This will modify the sound to resemble that of a flute. (See Sul Tasto below.)

Jeté (French) — "Throw" (bounce) the bow across the string to produce a series of short notes. Like skipping a rock across water.

Legato (Italian) — Use a smooth bowing motion with no break between notes except for the change in pitch.

Marcato (Italian) — Use a strong bold bow stroke.
Martelé (French) — Use a strong accented attack to the note with immediate release.
Martellato (Italian) — Italian for martelé. Use a strong accented attack to the note with immediate release.
Pernambuco — A wood grown in South America. This wood is considered to be the finest for making bows.
Pizzicato (Italian) — Pluck the string.
Ponticello (Italian) — Direct the bowing close to the bridge to produce a stronger sound. See Sul Ponticello below.
Punta d'Arco (Italian) — Direct the bowing to the tip of the bow to produce a softer sound.
Ricochet (French) — Bounce the bow off the string in a series of notes.
Rosin — Tree sap (resin) in a solid form applied to bow hair to make it sticky.
Sautillé (French) — Use a light bow stroke bouncing across the string.
Spiccato (Italian) — Use a bouncing bow stroke across the string to produce very short separated notes.
Staccato (Italian) — Produce a short note using any of the "separated note" techniques listed.
Sul (Italian) — Sul means "on." It is also used to indicate "near" as in "sul ponticello."
Sul Ponticello (Italian) — Bow near the bridge to produce a stronger sound.
Tasto (Italian) — The fingerboard.
Sul Tasto (Italian) — Bow over or near the fingerboard to produce a softer sound.
Tremolo (Italian) — Play the same note repeatedly by moving the bow back and forth rapidly with a wrist motion.
Trill — Fast back-and-forth changing of two notes a half or whole step apart.
Vibrato (Italian) — A repeated fast slight change in a pitch.

A Review of Violin Parts and Their Use

Back — The back of the body of a violin, also called the backplate.

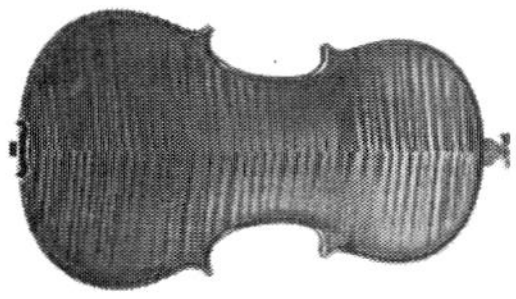

Bass Bar — A strip of wood on the underside of the top of a violin, reinforcing the top and distributing the lower notes throughout the top.

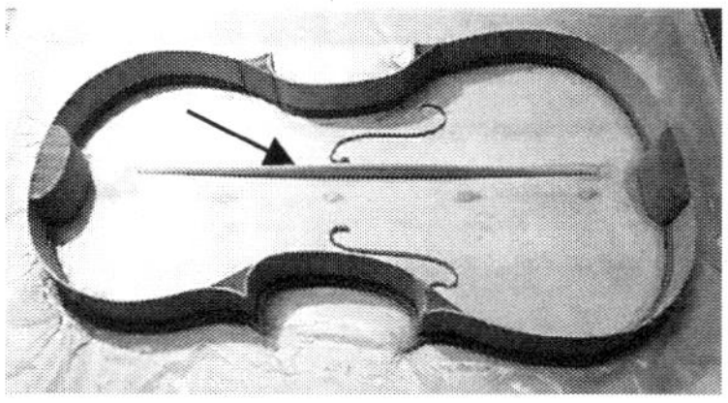

Belly — The top of a violin sometimes called the top plate.

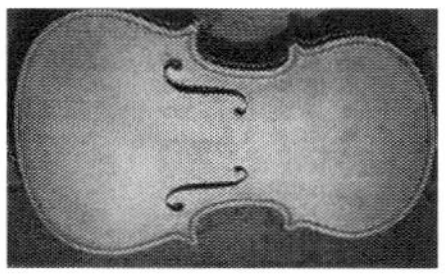

Bridge — A support for the strings on a violin. The bridge transfers sound from a vibrating string to the top of the instrument.

Bow — A curved stick made of wood or a manmade substance strung with horsehair or a fiberglass hair substitute. When used, the ribbon of hair is drawn across the strings of a violin to produce sound.

Bow Hair — Horse hair or a manmade substitute strung across a bow.

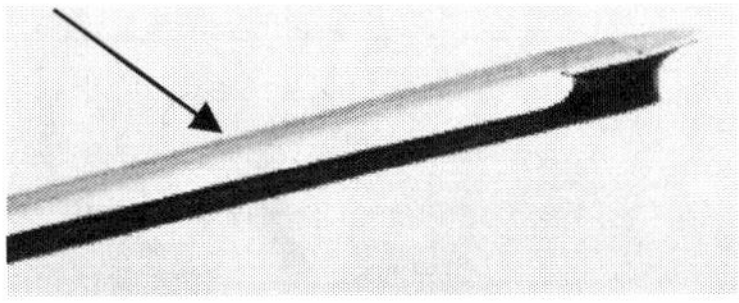

Body — The main part of a violin. The body (front, back and sides) strengthens the sound produced by the vibrating strings.

Block — A wooden block placed at key points in the body of a violin to strengthen the unit. One block is placed in each corner where the upper and lower bouts (see below) meet the C bout. One block is placed at the bottom of the body to reinforce the end pin and one block placed at the top of the body to reinforce the neck contact.

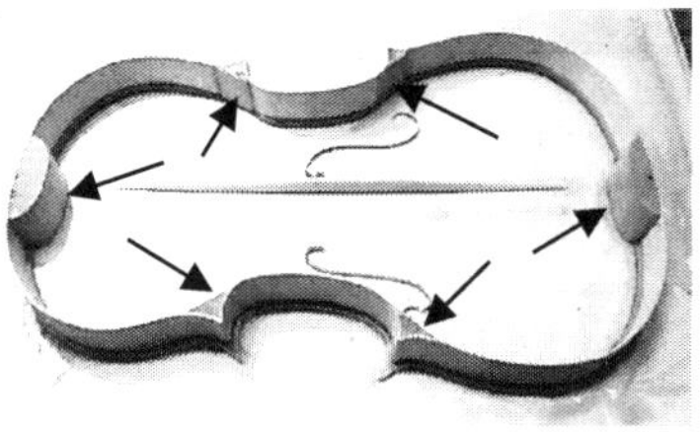

Bout — The word used to identify the three sections of a violin body. The upper third is called the upper bout, the middle section is called the C bout, and the lower third is called the lower bout.

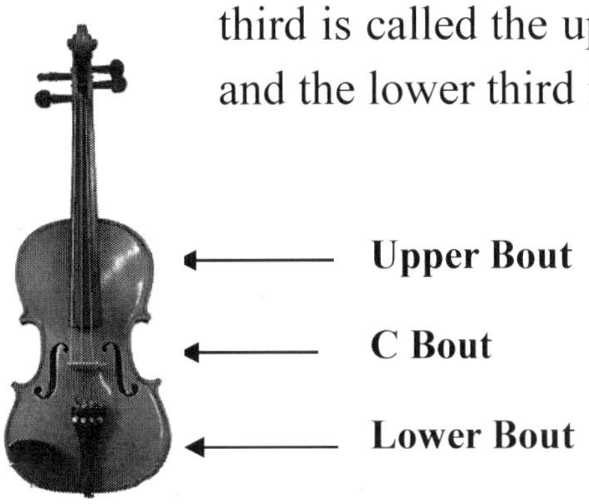

Chin Rest — A device designed to provide a comfortable and secure place for your chin while you are playing the violin.

End Button — A wooden wedge-shaped piece inserted in the end of a violin on which a tail gut is hooked to hold the tailpiece in place.

"*f*" Hole —Sometimes called a sound hole, an "*f*" hole is an "*f*" shaped opening in the top of a violin which allows the sound vibrations to escape from the instrument.

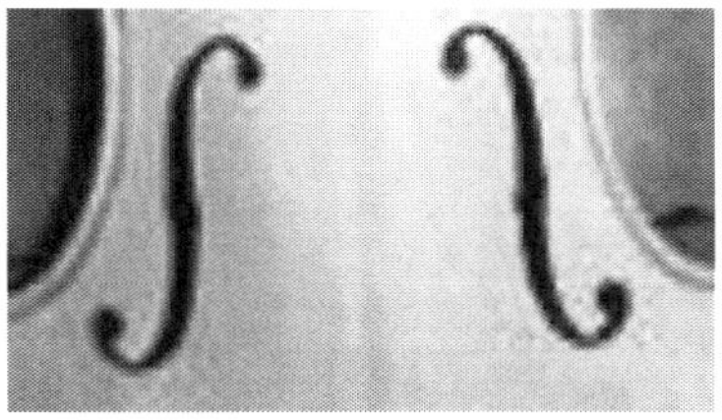

Fine Tuner — A device on a string or tailpiece that, when turned, will make a slight adjustment to the pitch of a string.

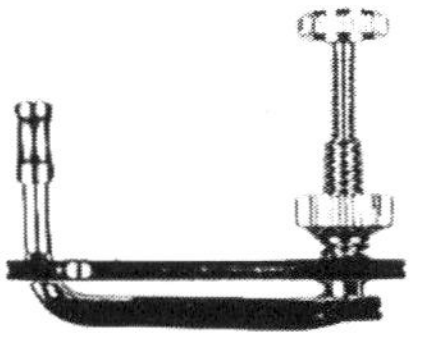

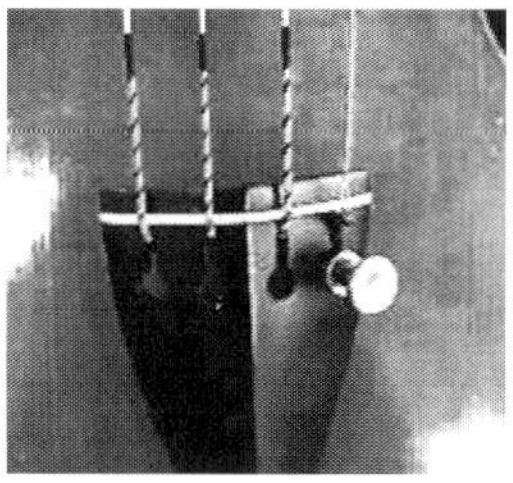

Fingerboard — A hardwood board (usually ebony) that extends from the peg box to provide a surface against which you can press the string to change pitches.

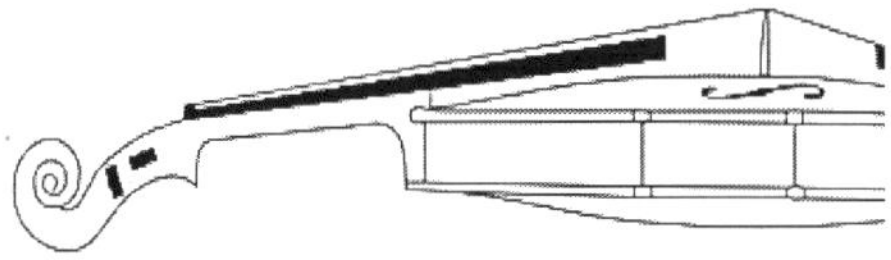

Lining — Thin strips of wood glued around the inside edge of the ribs of a violin to strengthen it.

Nut — The wooden insert over which the strings pass from the peg box to the finger board.

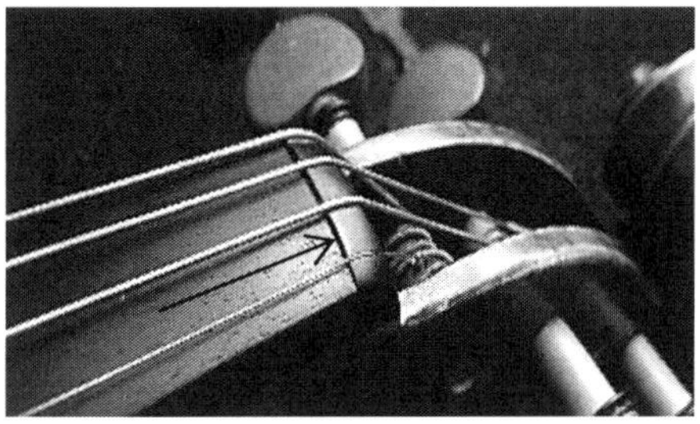

Peg — A wedge-shaped (smaller on one end than the other) piece of wood to which violin strings are connected to tune them.

Purfling — Two parallel strips of hard wood, usually ebony, inlaid into the edge of the top and back of a violin to strengthen the edges and control vibration.

Ribs — The sides of a violin.

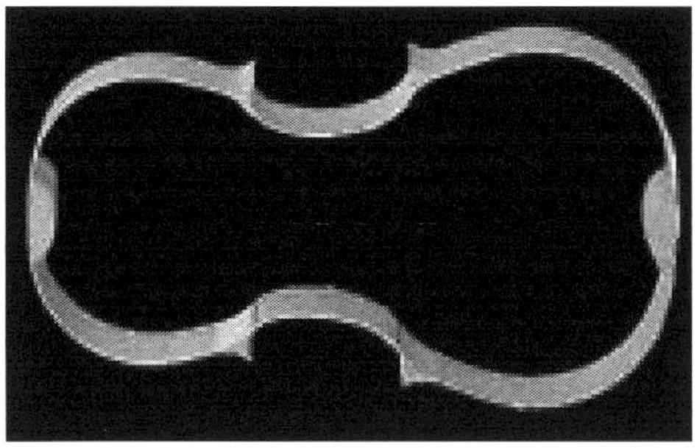

Saddle — A hardwood bar placed at the end of the top of a violin to support the tail gut and prevent damage to the body.

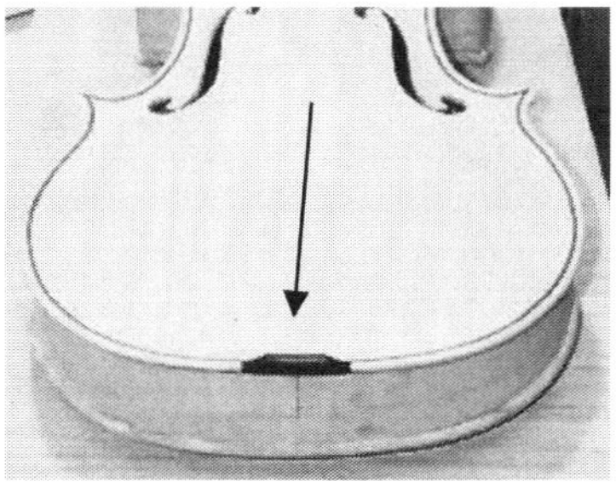

Sound Post — A wooden dowel (post) which supports the top of a violin and conducts the vibrations produced by the higher strings from the top of the violin to its back.

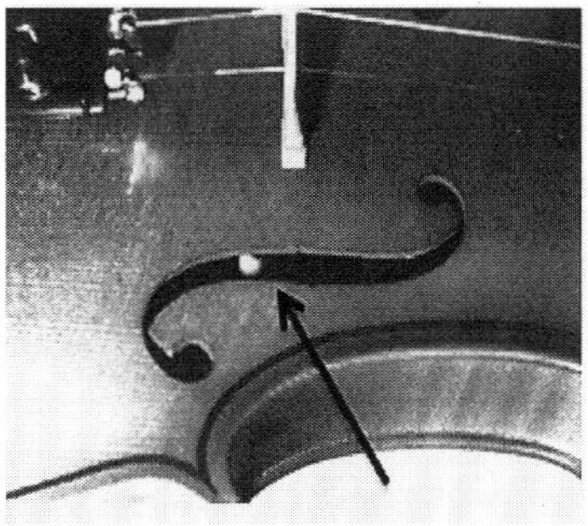

Scroll — The decorative top of a violin.

Scroll Eye — The center of a scroll.

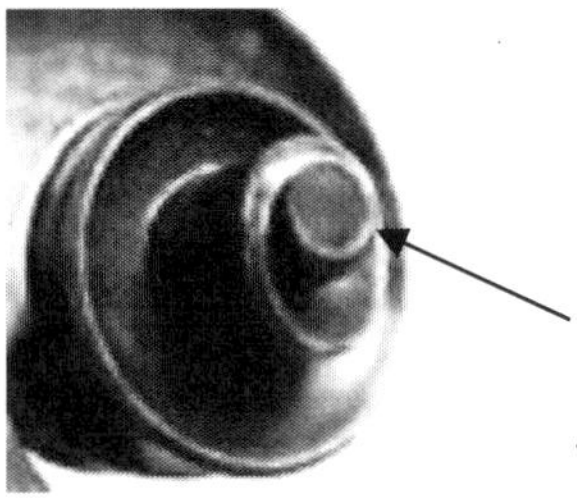

Shoulder Rest — A device used to help hold a violin in a proper playing position.

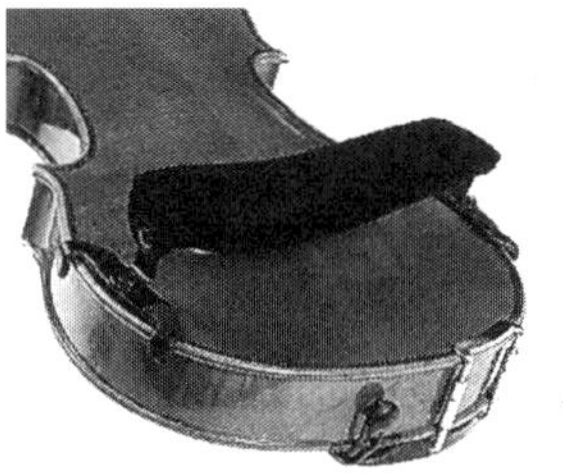

Tailpiece — A device to which the lower end of violin strings is attached. Some tailpieces have fine tuners built into them.

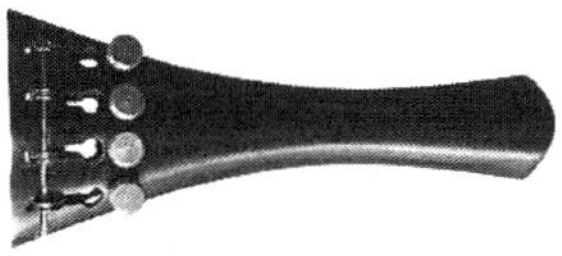

Tailgut — A short piece of gut or nylon that secures the tailpiece to the end button.

Index

accessories, 33-43
adjustments, 19-20, 27
Amati, 45-46, 69, 71-72
bass bar, 1-2, 4, 6, 52, 89
bow, 10-12, 17-19
  made, 75-81
Brescian School, 70, 72
bridge, 1, 3-4, 6, 19-20, 27, 45, 55, 58, 63-64
care, 17
  bow, 24-25
  cases, 25-26
  fine tuners, 23
chin rests, 1, 30, 37-38, 59, 91
Cremonese School, 70-72
electronic tuners, 7, 35
"*f*"-holes, 1, 3-4, 6, 20, 51, 64, 66, 91
ferrule, 11, 77-78, 80, 85
fine tuners, 7, 23, 35, 94
fingering chart, 16
finish, 17, 25, 59-61, 83, 86, 107-111
French School, 73-74
history,
  bows, 83-86
  violin, 63-74
horsehair, 80, 90
humidifiers, 42
kantele, 63
lira da braccio, 69
lute, 64
lyre, 63
  violin, 45-61
music stands, 43
mutes, 39
Neapolitan School, 70, 73
nut, 27, 56, 63-64, 92
open strings, 7, 35
pegs, 1,7, 21-22, 36, 45-46, 54-55, 57, 64, 66-67, 69
pitch pipes, 34
pitch, viii, 7-9, 13, 34-35,64
playing position, 30, 38, 94
plucked instruments, 63-65
purfling, 1, 5-6, 45, 50, 93,
rebab, 66-67
rebec, 67, 71
rosin, 10, 17-19, 25, 30, 33-34, 36, 40
saddle, 56, 93
scroll, 1, 8, 40, 53-54, 73, 94
setup, 56, 59
shoulder rests, 30, 38-40, 94
sides (violin), 1, 5-6, 45-46, 49, 55, 69, 77, 90, 93
sound post, 1-2, 4, 6, 51, 58, 93
spike fiddle, 67
Stradivari, 45-46, 71-73
strings, 27, 36-37
tailpiece, 9, 27, 35-37, 45, 55,

59, 91, 94
tuning, 7-9, 23, 30-31, 34-35, 50, 53
tuning forks, 34
Tyrolean School, 70, 73
vibration, 6, 34, 50-51, 83, 91, 93
vielle, 67, 69
violin,
made, 45-61
zither, 64, 66